SO YOU WANT TO START A FILM FESTIVAL

CONVERSATIONS WITH TOP FESTIVAL CREATORS

Strategies for Successful, Sustainable Events

Copyright ©2015 Jonathan Gann
All rights reserved

Published by ReelPlan Press, November, 2015
Printed in the United States of America

ReelPlan Consulting
916 G Street NW. Studio 203
Washington, DC 20001
reelplan.com

The views expressed in this book are entirely those of the interview subjects.

No part of this book may be reproduced or transmitted in any form or by any means, electronic or mechanical, including photocopying, recording, or by any information storage and retrieval system, without permission, in writing, from the author.

ISBN-13: 978-1519166654
ISBN-10: 1519166656
Library of Congress Control Number: 2015957077

ACKNOWLEDGMENTS

I could not have undertaken this project without the support of my friends and colleagues who guided me through.

Everyone should befriend a poet. Not only did the fabulous Kim Roberts edit the interviews, she organized weekly hikes to escape office pressures and provide a much-needed sound board.

A very special thank you to all of my festival colleagues and fellow festival creators. While the paths taken to our first events were dramatically different, and often filled with fraught—all achieved the success they envisioned.

And to Michael: you raise me up. Thank you.

TABLE OF CONTENTS

Introduction 1
Judy Laster — *Woods Hold Film Festival* 3
Nancy Schafer — *South by Southwest and Tribeca Film Festivals* 17
Laura Law-Millett — *GI Film Festival* 27
Kerrie Long — *Edmonton International Film Festival* 39
Jeff Ross — *SF Indiefest* 49
Lisa Vandever — *CineKink* 65
Nina Gilden Seavey — *SILVERDOCS* 73
Paula Elias — *Citizen Jane Film Festival* 89
Daniel Sol — *Holly Shorts Film Festival* 101
Sara Beresford — *EcoFocus Film Festival* 113
Elsa Lankford — *WAMM Fest* 125
Dan Brawley — *Cucalorous Film Festival* 137
Terry Scerbak — *Reel Shorts Film Festival* 147
Erik Jambor — *Sidewalk Film Festival* 159
Jessica Hardin — *Pasadena International Film Festival* 171
Josh Leake — *Portand Film Festival* 185
Resources 197

INTRODUCTION

So you want to start a film festival.
Why?
Close your eyes and ask yourself this simple question. Think long and hard—and when you know your answer, open your eyes and continue on.

If your initial response was "I love film and want to show how much I know," or "We need to kick start our economy, and a festival would be a good anchor event," or even, "It's cool!"—then put down this book and find yourself another hobby or project. I see events created with this mindset start up every day—and fail miserably after a single season.

If your initial response includes the words "passion," "community," or "fills a need," then continue on: you are already 80% there. What makes up the remaining 20%? Commitment.

A few times a week, I receive emails and phone calls from well-intentioned individuals who wish to create a film festival in their city or town. I ask them to complete the same exercise. If their answer lacks commitment, I thank them for their inquiry, and send them on their way. If their answer is compelling, I freely give my advice and experiences.

In 2003, I created the DC Shorts Film Festival because there was a void in Washington, D.C.'s cultural life—and a lack of resources for local filmmakers. I had just completed a year-long journey to over forty cities to present my short film at festivals around the globe. And in my travels, I was very disheartened by the majority of film festivals. Their preference for money and sponsorships over films and filmmakers left me yearning for a different type of experience. When I returned home, I knew I could do better. I had no idea how I was to accomplish this goal—only what pitfalls to avoid, and the goals I wanted to achieve.

I wish I had had a community of festival founders to call on, to hear their creation stories: the impetus for their events, the trials and tribulations of partnerships, the connections with filmmakers—and their mixed dealings with their boards.

This book is not a traditional "how-to" guide. In truth, there are over 2,500 film festivals in North America—and 2,499 ways to run them. Each event is unique, usually created by a film producer or director who identified a particular need in their community—and crafted an event to satisfy that need. No two are alike. How could they be, as each addresses different audiences with varying desires, film knowledge—and expectations?

Instead, this book of conversations with the creators of sixteen festivals—from the major pillar events of the SXSW Film Festival and Tribeca Film Festival, to small, niche events such as the Citizen Jane Film Festival or the Reel Shorts Film Festival—gives you insight into the minds of their founders. Some events were created to revive a sagging economy, others out of frustration for the lack of availability or ability to screen genre films, others to give struggling filmmakers their due by providing an avenue to connect to buzz-generating media.

Explore their genesis stories—and hear the honest tales of heartache and passion—and the lasting impact of their events on their communities, individual filmmakers, and the film industry.

Then read between the lines. All of the founders have one thing in common: commitment. The undying, passionate drive to create something truly wonderful, no matter the professional or personal cost. Their challenges and successes come with questions they never intended to answer, from defining and reaching their audience, to creating a system to find, evaluate and select films, to closing sponsorship deals, to ongoing board or staffing issues—and even the reality that their continued participation in the festival might come to an end—sometimes, not as their own choice.

And when you have finished the last chapter, if this is still for you—if you are ready for one of the toughest, but most satisfying challenges of your life, then get going. There is no need for you to start in the dark, like most my colleagues noted here. The appendix contains a short list of resources available for you. I provide a complete list of professional associations for festival organizers, media and submission engine resources, a 200+ item checklist of items to consider when planning your first festival—and even one-on-one consulting services are available at startafilmfestival.com.

Jon Gann
December 2015

JUDY LASTER
Woods Hole Film Festival

Judy Laster is a policy attorney and the founder and director of the Woods Hole Film Festival, as well as a filmmaker. She has been the Executive Director of the Festival for the past twenty-five years, leading its growth into the next generation. The Woods Hole Film Festival was established to promote independent film through an annual festival and other events such as a filmmaker-in-the-schools program, a winter film series, a filmmaker-in-residence program, and workshops.

So, Judy, I am asked all the time, "I want to start a film festival, can you help me?" The first thing I asked them is why, and unless they give me a compelling reason, I won't answer. I think that people don't know how others have created festivals. It's important hear the creation stories of small events, huge events, non-profits, for-profits — the whole range. People have no idea what is out there and what to expect, especially in the early years. And for quite a few events, the creators are no longer with the festivals — some were kicked by their boards, and some just burned out. I think these are important tales to tell.

I couldn't agree more. We do this because we love what we do; it's a passion and a calling. For many of us — and I've been doing this for a long time — in the early years we made it up as we went along. It's very complicated to put on a multi-day event with so many people involved. There was not big group of film festivals to connect with or draw from. Then, as now, you had to adapt because technology changed constantly and changed everything. Today, many festivals will learn by reading about their peers, which is great for them to be able to get an idea of the depth and breadth of ideas out there about how to run a festival.

I would agree, especially in markets that are already saturated with festivals and cultural events. Which leads me to my first question: what was your background before you started The Woods Hole Film Festival?

I grew up in Washington, D.C and thought that every city was organized around a central force like the Federal government, so, naturally I was interested in government. I was always interested in big picture issues and solving problems that affect people, and also in bringing people together and creating events. I've been doing both my whole life: I'm a lawyer by training and profession, but in college I took film classes, and have produced film and music events in my town in Woods Hole on Cape Cod, Massachusetts since I was in high school.

In the early years of the festival, people asked me, "Why Woods Hole?" I answered, "Why not Woods Hole?" There are so many people here who are doing so many interesting things that are world leading, especially in science, and it is a dynamic vibrant community. Woods Hole is a really interesting place because it has people who come here from around the world, who are very academic, very creative and who are maverick thinkers. This is also a community that's receptive to learning new things, and physically laid out so it's small enough to feel very intimate.

I started the film festival right after law school. My friend, Kate Davis (an award winning documentary filmmaker), who also grew up summers in Woods Hole, and I wanted to create an East Coast version of the Sundance Film Festival, which at that time was ten years old. We had each made a film and then we got films from five other filmmakers. It was a one-day, one-hour event and was completely sold out. Everything we showed was on 16mm or VHS. Interestingly, all of the filmmakers whose work we screened (Robert Stone, Bill Plympton, Robb Moss, Kate Davis) are still working in film and many have gone on to win many awards and nominations for Academy Awards. And so the Woods Hole Film Festival was born.

From that, it just sort of grew: first into a two-day, then a four-day, and finally an eight-day event, which is what is has been for a very long time. Kate went on to be a successful filmmaker, and I continued the Festival. In the early days, we were closely associated with the Coolidge Corner Theater in Brookline, MA for programming. We needed that because we were one of the first festivals in the area and because the web did not really exist as a place to share information about films. When we started, there was the Boston Film Festival (which has also changed a lot over the years) and that was pretty much about it in this area. Films were shot on film, shown on film, and people watched films in theaters. People quickly started hearing about the festival and finding out about it through word by mouth. And the audience grew along with the number of filmmakers whose work we screened.

As Woods Hole morphed into an eight-day event, it coincided with the birth of a film festival movement. That's when we started really expanding the outreach.

All of a sudden there was a platform to reach people and filmmakers in other parts of the world, and that changed everything. Now, in addition to the summer Festival, we program year-round screenings and present films in other communities throughout the region.

And the whole time I've been running the film festival I've also been a lawyer, working in the state government on policy issues.

What was the original mission of the festival?

The initial mission was the same as the current mission: to support the work of emerging independent filmmakers and show films by independent filmmakers that are of interest to people on Cape Cod, and to spotlight the work of New England filmmakers when possible. And because we're located in a scientific community, we try to show films that are relevant to the science that happens here at the Woods Hole Oceanographic Institution, the Marine Biological Laboratory, the Woods Hole Research Center, and the National Marine Fisheries Service.

When you started, did you have an audience in mind?

At that point, that audience was people that I knew in the independent film world, and the people who lived in this community. It was created as a community event, and it still is — it just happens to have a larger vision now, but it's still focused on creating community. The vision expanded because people have a broader view of the world than they did back then, and there are just more films being made around the world that are showcasing issues and stories that we may not know.

For your first year event, what was your greatest fear?

I had no fear.

Haha! This is why I respect you so — because you have no fear. So then, what was your greatest surprise then?

My greatest surprise was how hungry the audience was for what we were showing. They had to trust that what we were showing them was something that they actually wanted to see. They looked to me and the Festival as a curator and a presenter of ideas.

As time has gone on, and the speed at which information is made available to people sometimes outpaces our ability to bring them the films that they haven't seen otherwise, the curatorial and programming role has become even more important. Now, since films may actually play on the Internet, or create an audience before we ever show them, our audience knows about what to expect ahead of time. Now, we have the audience suggesting films that we might want to screen as well.

We start out every year with basically a blank slate. It's kind of like making a film with no script, no money, no actors, no anything except the expectation that you're going to win an Academy Award. That's a lot of pressure. To pull that off that every year is a huge challenge.

I think that most Festival Directors thrive on immediacy and problem solving.

Totally, problem solving. I can't even tell you how much the Festival has enhanced my life because I have learned about entrepreneurial skills that I never knew I had. And more importantly, I've learned how to manage issues in ways that I never knew how to articulate. I have really learned how to understand complex situations, and how to be a strategic and analytical thinker and communicator.

Working in the policy and political world, which is my full-time job, I've also been able to apply a lot of what I learned at the film festival to other issues. It's very similar, right? It's all about communication and creating a space where people feel like they can participate, and creating experiences for people who trust you and want to come back.

You said the first year was five films over a single day, Now, many years later, what are the numbers: films, filmmakers, audience, budget?

Last year, we screened 135 films in five venues to an audience of between 4,000 and 5,000 people. For the past few years, we have fried to keep it to 130 films or fewer, and we try not to have films screen in more than three venues simultaneously. And we do this on a budget of approximately $130,000.

Your organization is a registered 501(c)(3), right? Tell me about that process. How many years into did the event did you file, and what was the decision to become a non-profit?

Initially, the festival was held as an event under the auspices of a local community organization. We used their non-profit status to be able to do what we needed to do. Gradually we grew to be too large for them to manage and they asked us to form our own organization. It was a little tumultuous, because again, there were relatively few other film festivals to look to as a role model. We had to forge that path alone. I don't think there was ever a discussion about being a for-profit versus non-profit because there are so many things that we would not be able to do otherwise, such as getting grants and taking donations, both of which are critical to our budget.

I don't know how you would run a for-profit film festival because I don't know how that model works. I don't think this village would support us as much as if we were a for-profit venture. That being said, running a non-profit organization has its challenges. In my opinion, it is a crazy model for non-profits to have to have a board structure that is so time consuming to maintain.

Talk me about your first board. How did you find board members, and what were your expectations of them?

The first board members were members the community that I knew. Some are still on the board. I tried to get a combination of people who had the skill sets that we needed, such as attorneys, financial people and people in the film world. I had no expectations except to be there if we needed them. In my opinion, this is one of the most difficult challenges we face moving forward. We really do need to up our game financially. We provide a very strong product, and we now need the financial resources to compensate staff the way they need to be compensated. In the coming years, we will need additional board members and thankfully, there are people in the community who want to help us.

Another challenge facing the board is that I am both the Festival Director and the Executive Director of the organization, and those two jobs happening simultaneously. It is inherently inefficient, so going forward to we need to focus our attention on management and the Board. We will need to almost triple our budget to grow and prosper.

At what point did the event become a full-time job for you?

I would say during our tenth festival, when we went to eight days and to being our own non-profit.

Do you have any other paid staff, or is it just you?

We have a small staff of programmers, technical directors and marketing people.

During the year, we have one part- time administrative person and an operations person and me. The three of us work throughout the year, but during the festival, we expand to about twenty-five paid people, and about forty to fifty volunteers.

I have a part time professional job that I love, and which compensates me. Woods Hole Film Festival is my full-time love that compensates me by giving me a purpose.

Compared to many events, that is not a huge number of volunteers.

It's interesting…we're constantly back and forth about the volunteer thing. It's great to have them, and some volunteers are amazing, but some aren't. And there is a cost associated with that. I really don't know if it's better to have more paid staff and fewer volunteers. Some people who volunteer are very committed, and ultimately save us money and time. But when they're not, you have to back step to build redundancy into the system, which has its own costs, often more expensive than paying for staff outright,

Volunteers are always a challenge, because while they are well meaning, and you have to translate their goodwill that into productivity for you.

Over the last couple of years, something interesting has been happening. Because film is more ubiquitous, and high school and college-aged students are learning so much more about the motion picture industry and media worlds, many want to stay around here during the summer to work on the festival. They are smart, resourceful, and require less hand holding and on-boarding.

I think this corresponds with the increase in our reputation. As our reputation has grown, people are interested in becoming part of what we do. I think, in part, it's because we created a community that is really fun, and people really enjoy each other and the exchange of ideas. It's something that just doesn't happen to most people every day in their life.

You mentioned that you're not paid to run the festival. We both know the amazing

time and commitment that this endeavor takes. How do you juggle your personal and your professional lives?

It's difficult. I think about this a lot. It's a huge sacrifice to work this much and hard to make ample time for myself to deal with whatever personal goals and objectives I might have. Just last night, I woke up at 3:30 in the morning and decided to get up and start working. That's crazy and unhealthy. But I must like it, or I wouldn't keep doing it.

I also think it's because I'm naturally very competitive; not that I'm competing with anyone else, but I'm competing with myself. I started this thing, and I want it to be successful, and I want it to work. When you are the leader, this is daunting. I'm sure you know that too.

I agree. There's part of me that believes that waking up in the middle of the night and wanting to work for a few hours is perfectly normal behavior. My partner, and many others, would disagree. That said, I think it is critical to find that balance.

Right. Fortunately, I don't work this hard all year-round. Right now, I'm in my big crunch time. Not only is it crunch time for the festival, which is a few months away, it is crunch time at work too.

I've always been interested in the idea that people are defined by the work that they do. In fact, I believe that has happened to me. I don't really know what I would do if I didn't have the festival as an outlet.

That's interesting, because I have been asking people about what if they no longer had their festival? Some are forced out, and others need to move on — but cannot find an exit strategy. Do you think you could ever get out? Or do you think, "This is what I want to do forever"?

Well, I would like to be able to have a situation where somebody could step in and run the festival operations, and I can focus more on other aspects of the festival such as programming and fundraising. I'd like to have more full-time help. I've been trying to transition the vision to the next level and bring in a new generation: I guess that's the whole legacy-building thing. And even though I think about the transition, I don't have something else in mind that I'd rather be doing right now.

The situation you describe is very similar to where I have been recently. I am transitioning out of a festival I created. The process has been fraught with issues:

operational and emotional. This is an important issue that faces many film festivals, many of which were created by well-meaning people who love the work, the films, the filmmakers, and the community. But none of us planned on doing it forever.

It took a few years for me to finally get to the place where I could be OK with the thought that the festival might not survive without me. Or that it could grow into something I never imagined. Facing either scenario is a challenge.

> Of course it is. I try to remember what's important in life, which is relationships with people, your family and your friends. It's very hard in an organization that you've built out of your blood, sweat and tears to imagine not being involved. That's why they call it "Founder's Syndrome."
>
> A few years ago, a board member tried to take over the festival. Often people look at something that is successful and think about what they could do differently or better if they were in charge. That was the case with this board member. The rest of the board was outraged over his behavior and he stepped off the board, but the incident made me step back and look at the organization and my role in it a little differently. The Festival takes place in a small town, with a worldwide reputation, and my relationships go back many years. It's complicated to navigate something when there are competing interests and ideas.

After that first festival, how did you develop your programming style?

> I really learned a lot from other people, especially David Kleiler, who led the battle to save the Coolidge Corner Theater in Brookline, Massachusetts and who is recognized as the "Godfather of Film" in the Boston area. He has an incredible wealth of knowledge, and gave me great insight and an introduction into the programming world. By attending other festivals, I became more confident in my ability to choose selections that I knew the audience would like. Over time, I have really developed an intuitive sense about the audience that I don't think anybody else has. I can really read each film and determine whether or not it's something that's going to be a huge hit. I'm almost always right, which you hope is the case after twenty-five years. Of course that does not mean that everyone will like every film we program.
>
> Ultimately, our programming has to be geared toward the community we're located in. I feel a sense of responsibility to develop a program that's going to be both interesting and unique. That's why it takes us the entire year to develop our program.

Over the years, what other programs or initiatives have you started that really stood out — or may not have been as successful as you wish?

About ten years ago, we started a filmmaker-in-residence initiative and that has been hugely successful. Each year we invite three filmmakers who have a significant body of work, or worked on something significant in the independent film world. They'll show one or two films, do a master class, and serve as a mentor for other filmmakers. It has been successful, and I think it's one of the best things we do.

We started a Kid's Day program a number of years ago. It's a little harder to find films for this program because we don't receive many appropriate submissions. One year we partnered with NASA for the Kid's Day program because there was an astronaut on the space station whose sister lives in Woods Hole. Now NASA is my favorite agency. I would love to create the first film festival on the International Space Station, and they're not opposed to it.

As for programs that haven't been quite as successful, we used to do a staged script reading every year for the winner of our screenwriting competition. It was difficult because it requires so many actors to make it happen, plus, we did not get a big audience for it since it competed with the films we were screening for attention. After a few years, we stopped presenting a staged reading during the summer. We will relaunch that effort as part of our year-round series.

I always struggle with the questions, "Are we trying to do too much? And if we're going to cut back, what are we going to cut back?" It is important to keep our focus on the core program and mission. If it's something so extreme or in opposition to the festival, it just doesn't makes sense to focus our limited resources on.

Can you talk about your resources? Your budget is very modest — I would say about one-fifth of what it should be for an event of your size and scope.

We don't have huge corporate sponsors, which is a challenge for us. Local businesses are more likely to provide us with the resources we need. Unfortunately, much of their help comes in the form of in-kind donations. While in-kind is great, cash is critical to growth and survival.

In recent years, I have also noticed that people are becoming more interested in what they can get for free.

You think that's because…

I think it is a consequence of the changing world of film festivals and because so much content is available on the web and on demand. Films are becoming more expensive to create, and get out to audiences. Since ninety percent of independent films will never see a theatrical release, the festival circuit is their main avenue for distribution. Some filmmakers expect more "perks" in lieu of screening or licensing fees.

Audiences don't necessarily understand how much money it costs to present a film. Our ticket price has risen, out of necessity, to $15, which might not sound like a lot in a big city, but in a small town, it is significant.

It doesn't necessarily have to be in relation to the festival, but how do you define success?

Success is when you create an experience that's magical and authentic that would never happen without your input. Example: a few years ago, we had a film about Wavy Gravy, the announcer at Woodstock. He and his community lived in upstate New York, where they were part of every major aspect of the 1960s. He traveled here with the film, and it was just this magic moment for every single person in the audience. They were so thrilled to see him that they smiled the entire time. They were so supportive of him, and they loved the fact that this was happening in their community. It never would have happened if it weren't for the film festival.

I also love those moments when, a few years after seeing a film, an audience member comes up to me to talk about a film that may have changed their life. It's those kind of great moments that make it all worthwhile for me.

I agree. How do you develop your audience?

One person at a time. We have developed the audience by creating a good experience. That's challenging when you are working with a lot of people and a lot of different venues. It also means that programming has to be geared toward our vision. That doesn't mean everyone's going to like everything, but most people will like something.

What is your biggest challenge at the festival today?

Just one? I think we're at that level where we need to grow financially in a smart and sustainable manner, while continuing to operate.

In what ways has the festival exceeded your initial vision?

I think we've succeeded in becoming something that has its own life and persona. I never really thought it would still be going this many years later, so it's exciting. I love that I always learn something new, and I've befriended so many people from all over the world. It has broadened my horizons tremendously. What I did not expect was that it would become my life.

Where do you see the Woods Hole Film Festival in five years?

In five years, hopefully we will achieve the goals that I just discussed: being financially stable with a strong board and new management. That path could include an association with a university or other organization. Sometimes, I think it would be easier if we were part of a much larger organization, but it would be difficult to give up being an independent non-profit.

Do you think you could morph the organization into a for-profit model?

Somebody would have to explain this to me, because I don't understand how for-profit film festivals work. People donate a lot of stuff or give us a deep discount. If they thought we were running it as a for-profit they'd charge full price, which would be very expensive. Is yours non-profit or for profit?

I started DC Shorts as a for-profit, only because I bankrolled it for the first few years. When it grew to a certain size, my accountant told me I had to spin it off as a separate venture. That's when I had to decide between staying a for-profit or applying for non-profit status. I was warned against going the non-profit route, but was blinded by the thought of "free money." What I discovered was that grant funds were not "free," as they took a great deal of time and effort to acquire. There are times I question if I made a mistake.

The model for for-profit festivals — and there are very few in the U.S. — is that they were created with budgets so large that their money was never going to come from grants and donations, but from corporate marketing funds. From the ground up, they've been set up with very different structures and goals. Part of their business plan is to create ancillary outlets, such as distribution channels.

But since you're a non-profit, how do you fundraise through donors?

We have many wealthy individuals on Cape Cod, but they are also solicited by the many other scientific endeavors, social services, and a host of other arts organizations. Even though we are an established event, we work very hard to become more entrenched in the arts community both on Cape Cod and Massachusetts in general. That is also a lot of work, so you can't just be a single event, but an institution that does other things.

What aspect of the festival are you most proud of?

I'm most proud of the fact that it's grown into a very substantial event. We are a staple of this community. Last year, when Smithsonian Magazine designated Woods Hole as one of the top five small towns in America, part of that was because of the Woods Hole Film Festival. In my opinion, that's a big thing.

It is a huge thing.

We're a small festival, but we have a good reputation. At least, people tell me that.

You do and that's one of the reasons you're so highly respected. You created this organization over over a quarter century that is reliable, does not waiver in its programming, and provides the community that I think filmmakers are desperate to be a part of. Looking back, would you have change anything from the start?

I couldn't have changed anything from the start because I didn't know enough to change it.

But in hindsight, maybe I would have said to myself, "I want to do this for five years and then go do something else."

I have a goal, sometime soon, to spend a whole year traveling the globe to attend all the film festivals I can. I am starting to work on a documentary about festivals and the concept of community. I think it all stems from Woodstock: people create communities of choice, often through a cultural medium. We just happened to choose film. But the same thing can be said of other kinds of events: Burning Man, Bonaroo, there are festivals everywhere. How did that happen?

I'd argue that while many were created because of the need for a community, some of the larger and more well known ones were created by people who only saw dollar signs. While some of these events are important and create community, I do not think they have the organic or authentic spirit of those created from love. It's one of the reasons I'm putting this book together — to weed out the people only see profit, not promise.

What challenges do you see for the future of film festivals?

As the industry changes, as festivals compete with Netflix or online services for new and fresh content, I think we need to gain a better sense of where we are as a community of events, and to create robust mechanisms to support each other. I know that there is an emerging organization for film festival professionals, and that is a great start. We have to share with one another if we are to face the future head on. Especially one that seems to change almost daily.

Last question: Do you have any words of wisdom for someone who wants a film festival?

Be committed. If you're not committed, you're going to be miserable. And do it happily and go in with your eyes wide open, understanding what the workload is going to be. I would suggest learning as much from other people, make real friendships, become part of the community, and most importantly, treat people right.

NANCY SCHAFER
South by Southwest Film Festival
Tribeca Film Festival

Nancy Schafer is a producer who works in independent film. She is the Executive Producer of *The Battered Bastards of Baseball* (Sundance 2014) and Producer of *Transpecos* (2016) and *7 Chinese Brothers* (SXSW 2015). She is the Executive Producer of *Frame by Frame* (SXSW 2015) and *Come Down Molly* (Tribeca 2015).

Schafer worked at and ran the Tribeca Film Festival from its inception until July 2012, a period of eleven years. She was the Executive Director of Tribeca Film Festival (TFF) and the Executive Vice President of Tribeca Enterprises (TE). For the festival she oversaw all programming, budgeting and operations. Through TE she began and ran Tribeca Film, Tribeca's film distribution company. As a consultant, Schafer continues to work with Tribeca as well as other established and start-up film businesses and filmmakers.

Prior to joining Tribeca, she created and ran the South by Southwest Film Festival (SXSW Film) in Austin, Texas for eight years. Along with her festival experience, Schafer has worked on several films including two from director John Sayles (*Sunshine State, Limbo*); two from director Robert Byington (*Olympia, Shameless*) and began her film production career on *The Return of the Texas Chainsaw Massacre*. Schafer lives in Manhattan.

Before you became involved with the festival world, what was your background?

It was 1994 and I was only 23, so my only real background was college. I had volunteered for a few seasons of the Telluride Film Festival and learned a bit. Then I moved to Austin to work in film production, which I did for about a year before I was hired to start the film program at South by Southwest (SXSW).

Were you hired with other people to start the festival?

It was just me for the first few years. That's a little misleading because SXSW was already an existing music festival, so it already had an internal infrastructure. But the film team was just me.

So what was that first year like?

Nutty. I had no idea what I was doing. I had bosses, so I didn't just forge off on my own, but none of us really knew what we were doing. I would talk to people in the industry and I'd come up with an idea for a panel, or talk to people about movies. This was at a time where there wasn't a film festival on every corner. There was Sundance, and that was about it. Seattle and San Francisco existed, but they weren't household names. It was really just Sundance—and since it was 1994, it was not the Sundance we know today.

When you started planning SXSW, did you imagine the event would grow to be as big as it is today? Was that your intention, or were you just hoping to get something off the ground?

From the beginning, our intention was to create a powerhouse event. My bosses at SXSW had already created a huge music event that literally put Austin on the cultural map. They expected me to create something that would be long lasting. Two of my bosses had been film students, and their true passion was film, and they wanted to build a true film community. Between them and Richard Linklater, there was a lot of creative capital invested in creating this community and if you've been to Austin, you know they did!

Did you have a particular community or audience in mind when you started the event?

Yes, and I believe this is what all film festivals should do: define and find their niche. For SXSW, our starting niche was Texas. I reached out to people who had a Texas background, and that included a number of influential people, such as Michael Barker (founder of Sony Pictures Classics) who grew up in Dallas. But it was not easy to get people to come to Austin, even though the music festival was successful. I would mention SXSW to the film community, and they would just look at me with a blank stare. Starting Tribeca was a little easier because I would say, "My boss is Robert De Niro." That translates pretty well. But SXSW was an uphill battle those first few years.

Was it up to you to craft the mission for SXSW, or was one handed to you from your bosses? Or was there even a mission that first year?

I think we all crafted it together. The mission was very much based on the ethos of the music festival, which was to bring together the industry and the creative community.

The music festival was one of the largest music gatherings in the world, so the template was already there to create the film festival in a similar fashion. The music festival succeeded by scheduling the best acts. So we did our best to get the best films, and the best films would attract the best talent. I think that is still the goal of most film festivals.

As you launched SXSW in the first year, what was your greatest fear?

While I was probably most worried about programming, it was the logistics that probably most killed me early on. Programming is only one aspect of the event; you get your programming done, and then there's this huge amount of work that has to happen to get the whole event to actually come together. We just pulled all-nighter after all-nighter to get it to work. I can't really distinguish between years one, two or three: they were all equally painful.

Were you able to rely on South by Southwest's existing infrastructure?

Yes, so registration and sponsorship were all through the existing structure. That freed up my team and me to concentrate on programming and the logistics of screening the films.

What do you think were some of your greatest successes those first few years?

The film component of SXSW absolutely put Austin on the map as a creative place to live. In the 1990s, Austin was an amazing place to live, but with SXSW and Rick Linklater's Austin Film Society, it became a film paradise. Everyone was young, engaged, creating projects and working hard. It did absolutely what it was supposed to do: it created this incredible community. Of course, the city has changed. It is no longer an inexpensive place to live, and many of the creative community have moved on, but the core is still in place, and will be for many years to come.

Could you talk about the first year budget?

SXSW is a private, for-profit entity, and does not disclose financial information. But I can tell you that the amount was minute.

The for-profit model of film festivals is not the path most chosen. What are your thoughts?

It's interesting that I ran the only two major for-profit film festivals in the world. I've never run a not-for-profit, and I have no idea why people make their film festivals non-profit.

They see the pot of free money that is free.

Yeah, which is basically impossible to get your hands on.

How do you define success?

An amazing consumer experience. It has to be flawless, which means everything from the program to buying a ticket. I want it to be a really easy, friendly experience. I'm incredibly anal, and I am compelled to do a really good job. It's the attention to detail and the need for things to be done properly that drives me.

How did you decide on SXSW's initial programming strategy?

I was hired in November for a March event, so I didn't have a ton of time. I thought, "what can we get our hands on?" which is what I think most film festivals do. You know, "what's in our wheelhouse? Who supports us? How do we get their attention?" We showed films from Rick Linklater and Eagle Pennell, films from Bud Shrake and Bill Wittliff, who were both great writers. We called on people whose work we could use, and who would in turn could support us. It was a really a great way to turn out the creative community of Austin. It also supported our local heroes. I also had submissions the first year, and we did take a few films that were, as we say in the film business, over the transom. The years after that became less and less retrospective, and more about showing films that were submitted to us.

Was your job with SXSW full time from the time you started in November?

Yes and no. They hired me only to get through the first festival, but then I never left.

As the event grew, how did you handle the additional responsibilities while crafting the festival?

Eventually, I was given clearance to hire a staff, which is a radical idea.

What year was that?

I don't remember specifically when that happened. It was probably years three and four. They trickled in. In the beginning, I had seriously good seasonal staff. What happens with film festivals or any big annual event is that the seasonal staff gets to be so good, but they need year-round work, and often need to leave for financial reasons. Then you're forced with the decision to hire them year-round or lose a great asset. You figure out a way to keep those people, because they are valuable.

How did your staff play into strategic planning for the future?

Not at all.

So the big-picture decisions were done by you or your bosses?

My bosses and I planned together.

Was the decision to split off the multimedia track yours?

We happened at the same time then and still do. So they were both conferences happening at the same time in the same space in which you could cross over.

You ran one of the largest and fastest-growing film events for eight years. How did you juggle that with your personal life?

I started when I was 23. I loved everything about my job. I loved everyone who I worked with. Being in Austin at that time was definitely a heady experience. I don't regret a minute of it.

Frankly, it's something I figured out much later in life. If you want to have a real life, I would suggest not running a large annual event. I don't think I was very good at finding at that balance between work and life, that but it played into my workaholic tendencies, so I was fine with it.

Do you thrive under pressure?

God, yes! I do much better under pressure. I think all of us who run these big events do.

You look forward to the problem solving?

Yes. One of the reasons why I left Tribeca was because I knew exactly who was going to run into my office and what day. I had done it so long that the challenges weren't new to me. Sure, there are always challenges, but they weren't new challenges. They were the same challenges over and over again.

You took SXSW from an idea to one of the powerhouse events. Why did you leave?

The decision was tied to feeling that I needed a fuller life. I'm originally from the east coast, and I wanted to come back home.

Did you go straight into Tribeca?

No, I was a producer on a John Sayles film called *Sunshine State*. I lived in Florida for six months and worked on the film for almost a year.

The story of my move to Tribeca is actually very interesting. I moved to New York on September 8, 2001. Then the twin towers fell, and no one in the creative community in New York City had a job. We weren't supposed to have fun anymore. We weren't supposed to create works of art. So I was in trouble looking for a job.

Frankly, I thought I was moving out of festivals. I thought I was moving towards production, but no productions were happening. So when Robert De Niro and Jane Rosenthal announced Tribeca, I sent in my resume and got the job in February. I wasn't part of the team that created the business plan and mission, but I was on the original team as the first logistics person. The second the festival was over, I was hired year round.

If you were brought on board in February, and the festival was in May, you must have been a little crazed.

It was a crazy experience. George Pataki would stop by our office to make sure we were fine, because we were a symbol of this massive regeneration of downtown. For years, the mission of the film festival was to bring businesses back to downtown. We were the "great hope." It was a very heady experience.

When you walked out of our office and looked left, there was the hole left behind by the World Trade Center. When the days got too hard, we used to go outside and look left. We all felt that we were there for a real purpose, a civic and national purpose, not just a film festival.

How soon after the first festival did you switch to actually running the day-to-day operations?

I was quickly made the Managing Director. A few years later, I became the Executive Director. I just knew what I was doing. It was a natural position for me. It was fun because I got to start programs for year-round events, and work on developing relationships with my bosses and colleagues. I loved creating programs that would support businesses in Manhattan, and New York filmmakers. That was a really fun because I didn't get to do that kind of stuff at SXSW.

Did you take many of the systems you put into place at SXSW to Tribeca?

Yes, and frankly, I learned a lot from it. There are systems that were ingrained in SXSW's culture that were really a throwback to the music festival. New York itself presented a whole host of different problems. As soon as I learned enough, I understood that those systems needed to change. Some systems were not appropriate, and others were counterproductive.

Was it difficult to change that workflow?

Yes, but I think it was good in a many ways. As I said, it's more fun to have new challenges. I thrive on new problems to solve.

What was the rationale behind Tribeca being created as a for-profit entity?

Actually, Tribeca started out as a not-for-profit, but my bosses quickly figured out that grant money wasn't going to allow us to pull off a major film festival in New York City. It was marketing dollars. So the structure changed either before or after the second year. Craig Hatkoff spearheaded the transition.

What happened to the non-profit status?

The Tribeca Film Institute still exists and runs as a non-profit. The Tribeca Film Festival was spun off under a separate parent organization called Tribeca Enterprises.

In your first couple years at Tribeca, what programs did you develop that exceeded your expectations—or did not work?

There were many programs we left by the wayside. Frankly, some programs exist because there are year round employees and you need something for them to do.

I am very proud of many programs I created under the Tribeca Film Institute umbrella that are still going string, including Tribeca All Access and the Gucci Tribeca Documentary Fund. These are programs that strengthen the community of filmmakers, and many of the program alumni have gone on to do amazing work.

SXSW already had an existing sponsorship team in place. Were you part of developing a sponsorship team for Tribeca?

Yes. The great thing about Tribeca is that there was a sponsorship team to raise money. Part of my job as Executive Director was to raise money. I was in every one of those pitches making sure the money was coming.

Tribeca was lucky to have staff. I tell every young festival that you raise as much money as you devote the time to raise it. The more people you have devoted to raising it, the more money you'll raise. If you can afford a year-round sponsorship person, you'll raise more money than if you can't. It's not rocket science. It's exponential.

You've been with two major festivals and you've seen how the landscape has changed over the last twenty years. What do you think is ahead for film festivals?

I think festivals fill a very important niche, especially for regional theatrical distribution. The distribution landscape has seen a significant change over the past few years, and will continue to do so. People still want to see good, independent films, but they don't support a year-round marketplace that sustains distributors. Festivals allow films to be seen, gain traction, and hopefully spur international, online and DVD sales.

Do I think there should be more festivals? No. It's nutty how many film festivals there are. People enter the film festival game thinking they're going to make money, which is nuts. If you break even, you're very lucky. No festival makes money. None. People need to understand that.

How has the relationship between film festivals and distributors changed over the past few years?

My relationship with distributors is very different from other festivals in the country because my festivals had to be highly selective.

Well, both are premiere events, so the type of films and the pressures are very different from a regional event.

Frankly, there are more distributors now, and that's a problem for a big festival like Tribeca. You feel like you should be impartial and spread the distributor love, taking films from a good selection of them. That's not really the case, but you know, you want to spread the love to keep everyone happy. So if you're a festival like Tribeca, which is a discovery festival, you don't want your whole festival to be films that are about to come out in New York City.

What challenges do you see for the future of festivals, specifically regional festivals?

So many do not have adequate funding. The challenge is how they make money. I don't know the answer to that. Frankly, it seems to me like a losing game. Do I want them to continue? Yes. They play a vital role in the industry. I have two films on the festival circuit right now, and they are going everywhere. People are really supporting the films. It's great for the filmmakers.

What are you doing now?

I produce movies, which is even less money-making than film festivals! But, it's incredibly fulfilling. As I said, part of the problem with the film festivals was that I wasn't challenged anymore. The other reason why I wanted to try something new is because I got so high up in the organization that I felt removed from what I actually cared about: filmmakers. When you're tasked with raising a lot of money every year, that's your primary worry. The event supported filmmakers, but I didn't, personally. I felt removed. Producing has allowed me to spread my creative wings again. It's a pain and a lot of minutia. There are a lot of daily tasks. But seeing your works come to the screen is very fulfilling.

Expand on feeling removed from filmmakers. I think this is the unintended consequence of creating a successful event.

It goes back to the fact that my primary job was to raise money. I was always a programmer, but even then it is hard to support individual films when I was running not just the film festival, but the year-round distribution business. I didn't have time. I couldn't focus on the filmmakers, and at the end of the day, I didn't really get to meet them. They'd come to the festival and I'd say, "I'm sorry I never saw you," because I always had to wine and dine sponsors.

After many years of running DC Shorts, I feel like I'm in the same place. It used to be personally fulfilling to hang out with filmmakers and monitor how they were growing year-to-year. Now I feel like I never even get to see them, let alone connect.

What are you most proud of?

I'm proud of both festivals. They are a huge part of me. They are both great things that I'm very proud to have been a part of.

Final words of wisdom for someone who wants to start a film festival?

Don't do it.

Actually, one of the ways festivals can be successful these days is if they are seriously niche. I met a woman who wanted to start a film festival and I immediately told her she's nuts. Then she pitched me her concept, and I realized that she actually had a great idea. So she started the Illuminate Film Festival in Sedona. They focus solely on consciousness cinema. It is something new, and frankly, there is a ton of money in that community. Their audience travels, and will come from far and wide, offering many sponsorship opportunities.

I think there is an opportunity for niche festivals that bring together a community that doesn't feel empowered to come together themselves, or can't figure out how to come together. We don't need any more generic regional film festivals.

LAURA LAW-MILLETT
GI Film Festival

The GI Film Festival is the first film festival in the nation to honor the men and women in uniform. During May, National Military Appreciation Month, the GI Film Festival brings together Hollywood stars, senior military brass and great films to honor the American G.I. It's a week filled with lively panels, fascinating movies (fan favorites as well as world premieres) and exciting star-studded receptions.

Laura Law-Millet is a third generation military veteran who has served in uniform for fourteen years in the Army and Army reserves. She is a inclusive leader and seasoned project manager who has managed multiple teams in the areas of intelligence analysis, supply chain and distribution, sales, event production, film and television production, and film marketing and distribution. People know her as someone who gets things done and makes things happen.

So first, what was your background before you decided to start a film festival?

I served in the Army and Army Reserves for 14 years, and then I was in pharmaceutical sales—so absolutely nothing to do with film and film festivals.

How did the idea come about to create the GI Film Festival?

The idea came about from a conversation I had with my husband, Brandon, one morning. At that time, there were a lot of films coming out in Hollywood that portrayed the military in a negative light. Every time there was a military character, they were portrayed as a drug dealer, rapist or murderer, and I thought that those stereotypes didn't reflect the real people that I knew in the military. We brainstormed about the best way to try to educate the public on what it means to serve. Since people are moved by film, we thought, why not a film festival?

Brandon had a background in communications and PR and my background was in organization, leadership and sales. We said to each other, "how hard could it be?" Let me tell you: a lot harder than we ever expected. I honestly think that if we knew what it would entail, I don't know if we would have done it. After you get into it, you start learning from your mistakes, and through the years, eventually it becomes a little bit easier. But it was pretty tough in the beginning.

How long did it take you to plan your first event?

Almost a full year. I would say at least nine to ten months of planning for the first event.

And what was that first year like?

The first year was modest. We had approximately 85 submissions and we showed twenty films. I had every friend I knew handing out flyers and working ticketing, and every family member working on staff doing all the behind-the-scenes grunt work.

So you knew what stories you wanted to show, the image of the military you wanted to highlight. Did you have an audience in mind?

The obvious audience is military veterans, but this festival is also for people who weren't in the military. Even though we have a niche festival, in my head, it's for everyone. I know now that a majority of our audience consists of current military, former military, their family and friends. We're kind of preaching to the choir to some extent, and we'd like to extend our current core audience. These films are entertaining and inspiring for everyone—even if they do not have a military background. Anyone planning to start a festival should think about who they would like their audience to be.

What were some of the founding principles, the mission, of the event?

Our mission at the GI Film Festival is to preserve our veterans' stories and connect service members to society. We select and screen films that have at least one member of the military as one of the major characters, who has to be portrayed with respect. I'm not saying that they all have to be heroes and perfect, but if they do something out of character there has to be adequate consequences. Our founding goal was to educate the public about what it means to serve—in and out of the arena of war—in an interesting and inspiring way.

Sometimes in Hollywood movies, a Private will tell a General off, or curse him out, and then nothing happens to him. That would never happen in real life. So as long as it's an honest portrayal, we're happy to screen the film.

And, of course, technical proficiency is important, but not a deal breaker. Ultimately, we use the common sense rule: would you be happy that you paid $10 to see this film?

What was your greatest fear as you were planning that first-year event?

I don't think I had any fears the first year. Ignorance is bliss. In my head, I just thought, "Oh it's all going to work out. Everything is going to be fine." I think it's good not having fear, because if you have the fear, you probably wouldn't do it. I think you just have to go for it.

I think the second year, after I knew what to expect, my fear was that no one was going to show up. We collected these amazing films and great stories, but what if no one's going to see them? That's still my greatest fear, even after nine plus years. Luckily, people keep coming back year after year. These films move them and we have a loyal fan base.

Across the board, it's everyone's greatest fear. You are in good company. What was the greatest surprise or unexpected outcome from your first event?

Definitely getting some celebrity support. I was just surprised that with no track record and just an idea that we were able to reach out to people who knew people who knew people—and ended up hosting a few celebrities. That was very surprising.

I don't know if this is true for everyone, but because we have a specific cause and there are several celebrities who support the troops and support independent filmmakers.

Trust me, that is surprising. I think that with the exception of the big festivals and a few niche events, arranging for current celebrities to attend is not so easy. In fact, of the dozens of film festivals in Washington, DC, GIFF is probably the most celebrity-studded event.

Wow—that's interesting to know. I just assume all the other festivals are doing the exact same thing, but maybe that's not the case.

You mentioned that you screened 20 films in your first year. Tell us about the last festival: number of films, days, and venues.

We've grown from a three-day event with twenty films to a seven-day event with 65 films at three locations, a theater in DC, a theater in Fairfax, Virginia and an embassy in DC. Our primary festival is in the Spring in DC and we also host a West Coast GIFF for five days that showcases 35 films at five different theaters.

Are you set up as a non-profit or a for-profit organization?

We're a non-profit. We incorporated as a non-profit in 2006, and we held our first festival in 2007. It was pretty easy. We used Legal Zoom and completed the paperwork online. Two or three months later we were approved.

I think the process is much slower now. I've read in the newspapers that nonprofits are finding it harder and harder to get approved. Although there are a lot of benefits for incorporating as a for-profit. With non-profits you have to answer to boards but you can apply for grants. GIFF receives a lot of our funding from marketing dollars versus grant money or charitable dollars.

I think corporations' philanthropic divisions don't fully understand yet the power of film—the power of this art form to heal, educate and inspire. The connection has not been made about how film serves a philanthropic cause. If someone had a choice between building a house for veteran or providing a limb for a wounded veteran, they're going to give the money to that direct cause versus a film festival. Yet, while those are all great causes, film can also provide uplifting therapy for those who watch them or participate in the process of making them.

Hence, we receive our funds from marketing departments, who want to receive branding in a community event.

From speaking to many founders, I think that in hindsight, many feel that the non-profit path was maybe not a perfect long-term plan. That said, they also have no idea how hey would be structured or work as a for-profit.

I would agree. Although there seems to be success in the Sundance model where there is a partnership between a non-profit institute and a for-profit business.

Since you are a non-profit, you have a Board. How did you select your first Board members?

We have an extensive advisory board and a smaller organizational board. We selected our board members from people who have an interest in what we are doing and who have the connections and desire to help us grow our organization.

You come to festivals from a sales background. Has "selling" the festival been difficult for you?

Yes, it's different. When I was in pharmaceutical sales, I'd go to a doctor or a hospital and tell them here's the choice of two different drugs and here's why our drug is better. Both drugs will work, but here's why I think our drug is better and why you should use this drug. So they know what they're getting.

Now, when you're selling sponsorship and marketing benefits for a festival, you're going to someone who doesn't know that they need this. You're trying to convince them that they need to participate and why. It's a tougher sale.

At least you have the skill set. Many people who get into festivals have no sales experience whatsoever, and are surprised that their passion is not enough of a sales tool.

I guess that's true. Then I would say for those events, they need to find somebody with sales experience—or any other skill set they're missing. Passion and drive can only get you so far—you must actively recruit someone to join your team who has the skills that you're missing. If you have a creative type on the team, find a business organizational type. If you are a business organizational type—find a salesperson type. I think all successful festivals need a creative person, a sales person, an internal organizational person and an external business management person. In many cases one person will wear multiple hats.

So going into year ten, what is your approximate budget for the event?

Our D.C. budget's around $750,000.

That's a good, medium-sized festival.

You'd be surprised at how much we do on such a shoestring budget. During the festival, we have ten part-time paid team leaders and over one hundred volunteers. We try to get as much as we can donated in in-kind support to lower the cost of the actual event. Printing, venue rentals, party catering, and celebrity travel; it all adds up. Fortunately for us, all of our celebrities have come to the festival for free, and we didn't pay an appearance fee.

So it's not a lot, and to be where we'd like to be, we need a lot more money. We have a lot planned for the future but we need to be at a $1.5 million dollar organization.

At what point did this become a full-time job for you?

I would say it became full-time in year six. I'm really the only person who is full-time. Everybody else is part time and seasonal. I'm fortunate that I have a husband who has consulting work outside of the festival, because if it were just me today, we wouldn't be able to live in the DC area.

You mentioned that you are thinking about the future. What is your strategic process like? Is it easier or more difficult with only three Board members?

In a larger organization, you have one group that's tasked with focusing on current operations, and another group that's tasked with working on future operations, so when it comes to strategic planning, you've always got someone looking ahead.

Because we're so small and currently don't have the funds for a bigger staff, Brandon and I are handling current operations and then in our spare time we try to contemplate the future. That's just not the way for any organization to run successfully in the long term. You really have to think ahead.

You have a young family. How do you juggle your festival life with your personal life?

There is probably no separation. Brandon and I have an eight-year-old daughter who thinks she's a festival intern. If you were to come into our house right now, you would see festival boxes everywhere—T-shirts and catalogs and what not. There's very little separation, and that's a problem.

I would like to separate my private life from my festival life, but it's one of the things that you can't turn off if you want the festival to be successful. Unless you're able to grow to a point where you've got people who are working full time who are constantly thinking about things so that you don't have to, you don't have that luxury to have the time to turn it off.

We do try to take vacations and carve out "no work talk" moments in our lives, but those are few and far between. Luckily, we like what we do—otherwise it could be a much bigger problem.

You briefly discussed your initial program, you strategy. How has that changed over the years?

I think it's still similar, but we're evolving. We have had a lot more films in the last few years that deal with veterans' issues resulting from the effects of the current on-going extended wars: sexual assault, PTSD, suicide, some of these more complex issues we didn't cover in our first year. But those are the films that are being made, because those are the issues that are facing our veterans today. We like to highlight these issues and then show their solutions.

Initially we just focused on heroism, and now we've kind of evolved to showing the full spectrum of emotions and situations our veterans are going through. Even though we're showing harder-hitting films, we also try to focus attention on possible solutions. It's not just a film about the 22 veteran suicides a day, but the film will showcase some options for what we can do to help; here are organizations looking to help solve that problem.

As a niche festival, have you seen the amount of available content vary from year to year as veterans topics wax and wane in the publics' mind?

I hear of other niches that run out of submissions every year, but we don't. The first year, we had 85 submissions, and this year we're at about 300 submissions. I mean it's a relatively small number of submissions, but it hasn't gone down. It's increased from year one to now—and it keeps going up.

As a festival, we are also getting more respect from studios. If there's a studio film with a military component that's coming out around the time that our festival, that studio will ask us to screen it. That's kind of a neat thing.

How do you find working with the studios and distributors?

Studios and distributors can be tricky to work with. They always want what is best for their client's film. If a film has distribution, they will ask for the best screening possible for their films. So they will often try to negotiate for a better time slot, better marketing—you know, just better everything.

For films that don't have distribution yet, we are happy to work our partnerships with some distributors and channels to take a look at these films. We've been fortunate enough to help some of our filmmakers get their films on HBO, Showtime, Discovery Military Channel, PBS, Hulu, iTunes, and Netflix among others. Our ultimate goal for our festival filmmakers is to get a good distribution deal for as many of these independent films as possible and allow them play to a wider audience.

Does any industry personnel attend the festival?

Not in any organized manner. Usually partners we've worked with, such as PBS, American Heroes Channel, which is the former Military Channel, the Pentagon Channel, Cinemark Theaters and representatives from our media partners attend the festival or the after-parties where the networking happens. But our festival does not host a distribution film market. Most of the distribution partnership connections are done before or after the festival on a film-by-film basis.

Over the years, what programs have you implemented that have really hit it out of the ballpark?

We started hosting what we call Filmmaker Boot Camp, where we get speakers from different TV and Cable networks, producers, writers, and festival folks to talk to our filmmakers. The filmmakers have always said that it was their favorite part of the festival—to hear from industry professionals.

We call it a boot camp, but it focuses on all of the aspects of filmmaking after you develop your script: finance and distribution, getting your show on a network, getting your script produced, getting it programmed into festivals. That program has been a huge success.

Also, our festival started out as a film festival focusing on American stories, but over the years, we've received a lot of great foreign films and so we've added an international night to our programming, which has been extremely successful. We are now seeing more and more submissions from overseas. Audiences are excited to see military stories from countries around the world—their themes are universal.

Conversely, have you implemented any programs that have been less successful?

We started a screenplay competition two years ago. This program hasn't really taken off yet and is very time consuming. Every year, we tweak it a bit, hoping to steer it towards better success. It's too early to tell.

Tell me about your audience development plans. I know that you're trying to expand a wider audience. What are you doing to make that happen?

Probably not enough. I always feel like it's never enough. I think it may be where we advertise. This year we were able to get advertisements in the Washington Post, in addition to of our current media outlets: the Military Times, Stars and Stripes, The Hill Newspaper and other military media publications. I think we've expanded our audience by expanding where we advertise.

This year, we also expanded our definition of a military film in hopes of drawing in additional people. We've added a new category where the film can cover any subject as long as the director, writer, or producer was military. We had five films this year that didn't have a military component to it.

In 2015 we moved to a new venue in Northern Virginia—the Angelika at the Mosaic. The venue is state of the art and has tons of free parking. We advertised locally around the Angelica Mosaic Theater, in the Fairfax Times, and tried to partner with local community groups and merchants.

Talk about your move from downtown to the suburbs. Was that an easy move? Did you find that your audience moved with you? Did you lose some audience? Did you gain others?

It was a combination—a bit of all of the above. We did lose some. There are people who are hardcore DC people, and they are not driving across the river in any direction for any reason. We had been looking to move because the venues that we used in past are limited in size, and flexibility in scheduling. Normally, our nighttime screenings have 400-500 hundred attendees, while our daytime screenings will maybe have only 100. So moving to the Angelika Theater in Fairfax was convenient because it has multiple screening rooms of various sizes—smaller screens and larger screens.

So, while we did lose some of our DC folks, we did pick up Virginia folks, and a lot more veterans, retired military veterans, defense contractors. I mean those are our audience, and they tend to live in northern Virginia. They loved the new facility. So you know, I think it was good. I think we're going to stay in the Mosaic until we outgrow the space.

Was there a cost saving? Were there any other factors?

Having the entire festival in DC, all the hotels were extremely expensive. The hotels near the new venue are much less expensive—and newer. Fairfax is also closer to Dulles international airport, which makes travel to the festival easier for our out-of-town guests.

Everyone complains about parking. There's no parking in DC, or the parking that is available is very expensive. The new venue has tons and tons of free parking.

How do you define success?

Well, every year for the festival I would say success is a) having our sponsors happy and wanting to come back, b) having the audience say, "Wow, I love that film. I love this festival," and c) having our filmmakers love their experience at the festival. When those three key components are met, I feel good about the festival and can say we had a great year.

Overall organizational success would be having funds to hire three or four key full-time staff. I would be extremely, extremely happy if we could hire three or four year-round people who would each focus on their specific areas of the festival and I could take off a hat or two. Then the festival would be stable and would be a permanent fixture on our cultural landscape. That would mean success to me.

What are your biggest challenges right now?

I know I'm going to sound like a broken record—it's money. It's always money. It's being able to hire staff. It's building a team that's focused on growing the event and managing it.

Expanding on that, where do you see GIFF in five years?

Well, I see us having full-time staff. I see us growing and expanding our programming and event reach. We're now hosting an annual west coast GI Film Festival in San Diego every fall. We have partnered with Fathom events and will host theatrical events to 500 theaters nationwide. We're working on a partnership with PBS to bring mini-festivals to cities across the country. And we are bringing one night of content to military bases around the country. I see us doing more of these type of partnerships and events.

Oh, that's exciting. What are you most proud of? What DNA did you put into GIFF that you think would have the biggest impact in the future?

Wow, another hard question. During the festival I'll sit in the back of the theater and I'll watch people watch the films. Seeing their reaction—that is huge to me. It's so funny, it's not necessarily the money, or people saying, "great job" to me; I don't really care about the compliments, although I appreciate them. It's when I see people react to the film, that is exciting to me. It's exciting to see that, and hear from audience members how a film changed their life.

After a recent screening, a Vietnam veteran told me that for the first time in forty years, he cried because he saw a film that reflected his story. He said he'd never seen his story on screen before.

After another film, a woman told me that she had no idea what her son was really going through, and that the issues associated with PTSD were more far-reaching and personal than she ever thought.

Brandon and I just look at each other and think, we made these moments happen. We are changing people's lives. This is a powerful event.

That is powerful.

Hearing something like that is what makes all of the hard work worth it. Hearing these stories it's so gratifying. I think, "Wow, this is actually making a difference. We're not just doing this for our personal glory. People are making connections, and people are seeing stories and healing and connecting. That excites me.

What do you see as the challenges for the future of film festivals in general?

I think the biggest challenge is competing for people's time. There's just so much out there for people to do. You can binge watch a great show on Netflix all weekend, or there may be some other activity, or you can leave your house and go to the theater. It's really competing for time. We all have limited time, and people are very particular with their time, now more than ever.

That said, I really feel like you cannot replicate the movie-going experience. Even when you watch a film at home or on a mobile device, it doesn't play the same as when you're in the audience of a movie theater with others around you. People think that they can replicate that at home, but it's not the same. Convincing them that it's worth coming out of their homes and into a dark theater is a challenge.

And finally, what words of wisdom do you have for someone who wants to start a film festival—other than "don't."

Think about your skill set, and what skills you do not have. Be brutally honest. Then try to partner with people who have the skills that you're lacking. Don't think that you can do it all—very few people who can. Find good partners, people you like, people who you're not going to get sick of, and people you can respect, people you can trust who have the complementary skills that you need. Then just go for it.

KERRIE LONG
Edmonton International Film Festival

Kerrie Long has been heading up the Edmonton International Film Festival (EIFF) since 2003. She also works with her husband producing long-form documentaries, commercials, corporate videos and short films. Their company is Frame 30 Productions (www.frame30.com). Kerrie has won numerous accolades including the 2010 Mayor's Arts Award for Excellence in Arts Administration. She has served as a juror at the Banff Mountain Film Festival, Reel Shorts Film Festival, the Independent Spirit Awards, Canadian Screen Awards and the Student Film Festival at the University of Alberta. Kerrie has also been a guest speaker and panelist at events produced by Canadian Women in Communications and Technology, the International Film Festival Summit, and Canadian Public Relations Society.

Why did you create the Edmonton International Film Festival? What need were you trying to satisfy?

Edmonton's Film Festival was created in 1986 as the Local Heroes Film Festival, programmed in February and March annually. Over one week, it showcased twenty feature length films and twenty shorts, with a focus on films produced locally, in the province of Alberta (Canada). Funded and produced by the National Screen Institute (NSI), organizers would fly in from the NSI's head office in Winnipeg to be on the ground in Edmonton for a few weeks leading up to and during the festival. In 2002, the NSI decided to re-locate Local Heroes to Winnipeg.

A volunteer Board of Directors was assembled in Edmonton, which formed a not-for-profit, charitable organization under the Alberta Societies Act. That Board re-branded Edmonton's film festival as the Edmonton International Film Festival (EIFF), and moved it to the fall, placing it on the Canadian film festival "circuit" which starts with the Toronto International Film Festival and ends with Vancouver International Film Festival. I was contracted in 2003 as General Manager to secure funding and steer the re-brand.

What was your main passion or reason for coming on to a new event?

I had worked as a Producer in television and film for a decade prior to joining

EIFF and enjoyed attending the Local Heroes Film Festival. When the GM position was posted, I thought, "How hard can it be?" Twelve years later, I can now answer, "Harder than I ever imagined." In hindsight, it's probably a good thing I was clueless about the steep learning curve I had signed on for, or I might not have chosen to do so.

What is EIFF's mission?

To showcase films of all lengths and genres from around the world that Edmontonians may not have any other opportunity to see. To nurture local, emerging and established filmmakers.

What were your founding principals?

In my experience, film festivals are often thought of by audiences as "too arty" for most people. Many of the films are subtitled, and that intimidates some. So our mission in Edmonton was to debunk the myth that film festivals only screen "navel-gazing art films." We focused on curating packages of short films that would offer audiences a palatable selection of film choices. If they didn't like a film, they'd only have to wait a few minutes until the next one. These cinematic tidbits were an introduction to the quality of films we program and gave new festival goers the confidence to dive in and sample our feature-length offerings.

Who was your event for? Did you have an audience in mind?

Primarily, our audience is comprised of Edmontonians. We also work with schools to present films for students—future festivalgoers. And we are now seeing an increase in people travelling to EIFF from northern Alberta. Filmmakers are a huge focus for our event as well. We have to "wow 'em." They are the best ambassadors we have!

Did you have your community in mind when founding your fest?

Our community is at the top of my mind year-round. Where possible, we partner a film, or series of films, or a visiting filmmaker, or a school, with organizations whose members are interested in a particular film's content. As an example, with the short film *Down In Flames: The True Story of Tony "Volcano" Valenci*, we partnered with the Edmonton International Street Performers Festival and they spread the word to their database.

We also created a 24-hour filmmaking challenge to strengthen our own industry and a noon hour short film series, Lunchbox Shorts, to attract business owners and office workers. We like to think that we have our ear to the ground so that we're giving festival goers what they want, and more importantly, what they need.

As you prepared the first year, what was your greatest fear?

My biggest fear was that no one would come. We had a new name, a new time of year, and no budget to advertise either of those changes. And this continues to be my greatest fear each and every year.

What was your greatest success that year?

Our greatest success in that first year was convincing a handful of sponsors and funders to take a leap of faith with us. They didn't understand us or what it was we were trying to do, but they believed in our passion. This continues to be an accomplishment every year.

Did you have a failure, or an aspect of the festival that did not meet expectations?

I can't pinpoint a specific failure, however I do have one regret. In my first year, I had no media training, so I would talk to reporters like we were old friends. Sometimes I said things I shouldn't have said (even though I always speak the truth), and those words were printed or broadcast. I got into hot water with my Board of Directors on several occasions in the first couple of years. My one piece of advice to newbies is to work with a communications or publicity person. You are a key component of your festival's "brand."

So, tell me about the festival today. What are the numbers?

Last year, we programmed 150 films in 65 screenings at three venues. Our audience attendance was just shy of 20,000 people, and 65 filmmakers travelled here (mostly from Canada and the U.S.A.).

And your budget?

We perform miracles with just $600,000, which includes in-kind sponsorship.

What are your biggest challenges?

We are a small-ish city, with a population of just over 1 million. Considered "blue collar", many residents work in the oil sands which are located four hours north of Edmonton.

We are also a city that's passionate about sports—have you heard of the Edmonton Oilers?

We are also known as the "Festival City": Edmonton has more festivals in one year than any other Canadian city. I often feel that by the time our festival rolls out in October, Edmontonians are suffering from festival burn out. The kids are back in school. The leaves need to be raked. The air is crisp. People start wanting to hibernate. So it's a big challenge for us to lure them from their comfy couches and their big-ass TVs, tuned to their favorite sports channel…

I completely understand your concern. And I think that competing against home theaters, apathy and/or event overload is a big problem in many communities. With so many things to do, sometimes it is easier to do nothing.

What are some of your operational issues or concerns?

Sponsorship and funding. Every year, we have to negotiate and explain the value that our film festival contributes to the quality of life for Edmontonians. We are staring into the jaws of another recession here in Alberta. The first thing that big business cuts is everything related to arts and culture. Let's face it…we aren't saving lives here. So we continue to do more with less.

Future-proofing is another operational concern. There never seems to be any time (or money) to produce an exit strategy for me, personally. It is time for our organization to look at future leadership. It should be a priority, but when you are in the thick of planning the festival, that priority takes a back seat to the festival.

It is interesting that you mention an exit strategy. In speaking with many others, they want a seamless transition out of their organization, but have a hard time either figuring out what that looks like, or the Board is unable to define what makes a qualified candidate, or the action of inaction creeps into the process—and nothing gets done.

As we talk today, I am transitioning out of DC Shorts, and that process has been very difficult: a balance between emotions, logistics, institutional knowledge, strategic planning, and, of course, funding.

Agreed! That should be your next book.

"How to Get Out of the Film Festival You Started." I'll start working on that tomorrow. In the meantime, what are some of EIFF's most recent successes?

We like to hear what filmmakers and audiences have to say about our festival. As long as they're happy, we're happy. Surveys, audience discussions and anecdotal interactions all give us this information. The festival seems to make people happy, so in the end, all of the planning and begging and heartache does pay off.

In what ways has EIFF exceeded or not exceeded your original vision?

I feel like we're still trying to reach the vision that I started with twelve years ago. I want to see people committing an entire week to the festival. I'd like to see films in more theatres, all day and into the night. I'd like to see festival goers and filmmakers all excited about this crazy, expensive art form. Synergies happening. Musicians talking to writers talking to art directors chatting with actors who are talking to gaffers and editors. And of course, I want to see every film screening packed!

How do you define success?

Success will be the day that no one in Edmonton, when asked whether they attend the Edmonton International Film Festival responds with, "What? I didn't even know that we had an international film festival."

That is very lofty.

Maybe. But reaching for big goals means you have big successes. The opposite would be to ask me what failure looks like. To me, failure is the fear that none of this would even happen. That is what motivates us to keep going.

How did you decide on your initial programming strategy?

Our programming strategy is really more of a "keep-our-fingers-crossed" plan than a deliberate strategy. We know that we need content for the "tent pole" events: Opening Night, Awards, Closing Night, plus we screen the Cannes Palme d'Or winner and a couple of heavy-hitters, such as features with Oscar buzz. And other than that, we roll with the content that distributors and filmmakers throw at us.

Filmmaker submissions are also a massive component of our programming and our selection committees, comprised of more than fifteen industry and non-industry volunteers, who consider more than 2,000 submissions of all lengths and all genres. We look for films that inspire, delight and motivate. EIFF also curates shorts and features from other festivals, and programmers from other festivals often drop in for a few days to find gems for their own line-ups.

Over the years, what additional programs or initiatives have you successfully implemented?

Our most successful programming strand is called Lunchbox Shorts, which I created and launched in 2004. These five unique short film packages are programmed Monday through Friday during EIFF, are 45-minutes in length and are curated from submissions. Each screening features four to five shorts which starts promptly at 12:10pm and ends at 12:55pm—fitting exactly into a one-hour lunch break. And admission includes lunch. Each day's lunch is provided by an independent restaurant interested in showcasing their menu to the downtown business crowd. Lunchbox Shorts attracts up to 400 patrons daily to the festival.

Funny sidebar…Edmonton is divided by a river, creating the north side and south side. You can find all kinds of people who have never crossed the river. So when EIFF was the Local Heroes Film Festival, the films were programmed on the south side. Our downtown is on the north side, and we have slowly been centralizing all of our events to the downtown core. Don't get me started on the number of angry people that we've dealt with over the years. When I proposed to the Board that we program short films over the lunch hour in the downtown core, on the north side, they actually made a motion to keep the festival on the south side. I was not popular with the Board when I announced at the following meeting that I had secured a film theatre downtown, a food sponsor, and a cash sponsor to produce the event. Go with your instinct. It's the best compass you'll ever have.

Wise words.

We have tried several ways to program films made by Albertans. We tried short film packages spread throughout the festival. We tried a full day of Alberta programming. These are fun for the filmmakers, but we haven't figured out how to get audiences excited about indigenous content. The year we tried all Alberta content, all day in multiple theatres, festival goers told us they were "taking the day off from the festival." Maybe it's time for us to drop the labels; a film is a film, regardless of where it comes from, or who made it.

Projection, projection, projection. I cannot say enough about ensuring the best projection possible! We won't compromise projection. It's the cornerstone of what we do. That's why you won't see EIFF program into "pop-up" venues; we only screen in professional cinemas. If we want to be a 'film' festival, we better be damn sure that projection is our priority and that we test the exhibition formats before audiences arrive. Filmmakers attending? Make sure to test their film with them, in the theatres where their projects will be screening. You have their "cinematic baby" in your arms and you'd better be sure it makes a stunning debut! Imagine hanging a Picasso in a dark basement, from a nail, with no lighting. 'Nough said.

How did you evaluate a program like this to make the decision to continue or drop it?

I believe that it takes audiences five years to buy into new ideas. I always call Edmonton a "slow burn." If it doesn't work the first year, give it a few more years—they'll come around.

How have you developed relationships, whether with sponsors, filmmakers, or the audience?

Our approach has always been one person at a time. We try to have a representative of EIFF at other cultural events throughout the year. I am constantly building relationships with sponsors, reviewers, filmmakers and distributors. These relationships often take years to become beneficial to EIFF. But, like I said, Edmonton is a "slow burn," so things take time. I am patient.

If your organization is a non-profit, at what point did you apply?

The application process to become a non-profit society and registered charity occurred before I joined EIFF, so I am not intimately familiar with the challenges that were involved. I have heard that the process is easier than the one you have in the U.S.A.

At what point did the event become your exclusive full-time job?

The first six years, from 2004 to 2009, I was able to do festival work part-time and continue to freelance as a Producer/Production Manager. In 2010, as the workload increased, I had to stop taking on freelance work. Years later, I am still figuring how to make ends meet with only the income from EIFF. I know our budget sounds large to some events, but our expenses are very high: venues, screening fees, marketing. Salaries, sadly, are rather low. But then again, little is better than nothing, and nothing would mean that EIFF would become a distant memory.

That's a predicament felt by most festival people who work for smaller events.

This is not an industry to get into if your goal it to make buckets of money. It is an industry you have to love.

Is your staff or Board involved in the strategic planning for your organization?

When I joined, our Board of Directors was hands-on, with very mixed results. With my recommendations and guidance, the Board is now a governance Board and does not participate in day-to-day operations. I have two part-time, year-round staff who help with programming, administration and wrangling our screening committees. At festival time, we hire approximately 18 part-time contractors.

I know you have a family. How do you juggle your personal and professional lives?

I don't. EIFF is all consuming for me. But that's only because I allow it to be. While we are chatting on a gorgeous Saturday morning, I've got a film submission playing on a laptop, which I will need to re-watch since I am having difficulty talking to you and watching at the same time. Meanwhile, my husband is cutting the grass and four of our six children are out at the Pride Festival. The other two are shooting a short film with our 35mm film gear (my husband owns a film company). I have to figure out how to juggle all of this before everyone I love no longer asks to hang out with me.

Looking back, what elements would you have changed from the start?

I would have preferred to start with a clean slate instead of inheriting a film festival with an 18-year history. Expectations by filmmakers, audiences, and sponsors were entwined with the festival-that-was. Coming in with a fresh face, new ideas and a unique perspective would have been so much easier if I'd taken the reins and ran with my own vision rather than trying to keep the "old guard" happy and shake things up at a much slower pace.

What challenges do you see for the future of film festivals?

Staying relevant. We're all questioning this, of course. Baby boomers get it. They still flock to movie theatres for the shared experience of watching a film, in a dark theatre, on a big screen, with complete strangers. It's the next generation we need to focus on. Almost everything is available to watch online. So how do we convince them that film festivals are a unique experience where they can immerse themselves in diversity, meet filmmakers face-to-face and widen their social network? I refuse to believe that the next generation is not interested—we just have to figure out a way to engage them.

For us, we work with Junior and Senior High Schools to program films during the school day. We call this program strand EIFF U—get your education in the seats—and this year more than 1,000 students attended and many of them expressed how they look forward to a field trip to EIFF every year. There's our next generation.

What aspect of the festival are you most proud of?

I'm always proud of our team when I stand next to a filmmaker following his or her screening and he or she says, "This is the best projection I have ever seen for my film," or "I have never seen so many people out, at noon, on a weekday, watching short films."

I am most proud of the filmmakers whom we inspired to launch careers in television and film. One of our filmmakers was just 16 years old when we presented his first short film. He is now in his early twenties and just took his first feature film to Cannes. His father, on the other hand, laughingly tells me that he wishes I had encouraged his son to become a doctor or a lawyer. "Can people make a living making movies?" he asks.

Successful ones do. Finally, what are some words of wisdom for someone who wants to start a film festival?

Listen. Always listen. And be thankful. When a festival goer complains—and someone will—remind yourself that they are telling you these things because they care. Otherwise, they wouldn't say anything, and you will have lost them for life.

Roll with the punches. A BluRay or DCP might stop partway through the film. You will forget a sponsor logo on your posters. The opening night D.J.

arrives five minutes after you need him or her. Laugh: our lives are all about surprises.

And after the crowds have gone, the filmmakers have said goodbye, after you've done your final reports and paid all the bills, gather your team around and have them all share their festival moments. Discovering those special moments make it all worthwhile.

JEFF ROSS

SF IndieFest
San Francisco Documentary Festival
Another Hole in the Head Film Festival

San Francisco IndieFest Founder and Director Jeff Ross has produced events for over twenty years, ranging from nightclub shows, underground music events, art openings, live music, performing arts and film festivals. Now entering its 18th year, the SF Independent Film Festival draws crowds of over 11,000 and continues to support and celebrate maverick filmmakers and their work. IndieFest now presents three annual two-week long film festivals, the other two being the SF Documentary Festival and a genre fest called Another Hole in the Head. He has since produced over forty film festivals and seven music festivals, in addition to numerous arts shows, live theater, and regular one-off events under the IndieFest banner.

What led you to create SF IndieFest?

I was a club promoter in college and after, and had promoted some big live shows and a couple of art shows. I decided to do a short film screening in a bar venue; it was a disaster. At the time, I didn't know anything about film. This was the mid 1990s, so we were showing 16mm and video, formats I did not really know anything about. Anyway, for some reason, I got the bug. The following year, I walked into the office of the San Francisco International Film Festival to see about interning or volunteering. Their front desk person had just quit, so they gave me the job of answering the phones. All of a sudden, I was one of eleven year-round employees of the San Francisco Film Society. After a while, I became office manager, and then I became their operations manager. They only did one event a year, in the spring, so in the off-season, there was absolutely nothing to do.

The other staff members were either out raising money or driving around looking at films—and all I had to do was research copy machines. I had been a parking valet in college, and had kept that job at night while I worked at SF Film Society, as non profit arts work doesn't pay very much, as we all know. One of my co-workers there had a feature film that year at Slamdance and he couldn't get it played anywhere in San Francisco. The San Francisco

International screened the best films from all over the world, and while Rand's film was good, it wasn't "one of the best films in the world that year" good. Art house theaters were just showing films from the studios; they weren't doing independently touring films. I figured there were probably more people like him out there with films and no place to show them. So I launched a festival.

Had you ever attended an independent film festival before then?

There was no such thing in San Francisco at the time. In the mid-1990s we had some pretty well established film festivals, the San Francisco International being the biggest one, followed by the Frameline LGBT Festival, the Asian Film Fest, Jewish Film Festival, that sort of thing. But there were only about eight at the time, and I hadn't been to any of these film festivals before I decided to do that little short film program.

What were some of the founding principles of the festival?

Basically, it was supposed to be the home for wayward children—the films that were falling out of other places. Initially, we only showed feature films, because I just didn't have the way at all to deal with shorts. I guess we were just looking for whoever wanted us to show their movie. We called for entries, sent out notices for universities to post on bulletin boards, and people started to send us their movies to consider. They were all small, low-budget films—definitely that sort of "Indiewood" thing from the '90s. We didn't have litmus test, or say, "You have to be under this budget," or "You have to be a first time filmmaker"; we didn't have rules so much. I would know it when I saw it.

Until about ten years ago, in almost every interview I did, someone would ask me, "So what is independent; what does that mean?" because at the time, "independent" didn't mean anything. I remember at the time George Lucas was going around claiming he was an independent filmmaker because his films were all self-financed, which is absurd, though, technically I suppose it's true—he was working outside of the studio system. Then there was the rise of Miramax and by that point, the whole idea of what is independent didn't really make sense anymore, except for the fact that I felt like I knew what it meant when I saw it.

Did you have an audience in mind?

Yes, I certainly did. Since I was a club promoter before this, I thought the audience of people who are going to live music and live theater and DJ events would come to see films if they were presented to them in the same sort of way. I marketed it with club flyers, telephone pole postings and a chilling graphic. I was aiming for the 20-something slacker audience: the same people who were going to underground artsy theater.

That's not our audience anymore, because there are not that many of those people left in San Francisco except me and some people I'm friends with. There are not that many of those people left in San Francisco anymore, except some die hard artsy folks with rent-controlled apartments.

What was the first year like?

Exhausting. The first year I financed the festival with a bunch of credit cards. People kept sending me credit card applications, so I filled them all out, which I was proud of. I still am, because most of the films that we showed were probably financed that way. I'd say we had a budget of about $20,000, but, having never done this before, I was just making it all up as I went along and we ended up spending about $20,000. I should note when I say "we" I mean "I." I was the sole person doing everything except for the graphics, because I didn't know how to do that, so I allocated it to a woman who had just started a graphics design firm and had an office right above the restaurant where I was a valet. Anyway, I did everything to do with publicity: picking the films, getting the theater and marketing the festival.

I knew a fair amount about film festivals at the time, having worked at the San Francisco International for one or maybe two festivals by then. I picked up quite a bit about how they do things and extrapolated how it would work for a much more modest scale. I would scoop up some of their hardcore, long-time dedicated volunteers, who were literally a group of five or six little old retired ladies. That was my theater staff, but they had done film festivals so long that I could hand off all the theater stuff to them. I just did the rest of it myself, and it was exhausting. I remember one weekend in this theater I used. It had a balcony and I have memories of lying on the floor of it trying to close my eyes and rest while the movies would all play, but I couldn't actually fall asleep because I had to be up when it was over and deal with stuff like Q&As.

What was your greatest fear that year?

That no one would come. Then I'd be out, and in debt to the credit card companies. Every event I've ever done I have always been afraid that no one will come and I'm going to lose my shirt. They're all still financed and I'm not insanely wealthy, so that's always been my biggest fear: that it's not going to work. The other fear, which I've developed since, is the sense that a bad turnout will look bad for the filmmaker. I feel like the only real job a film festival has is creating a good audience for the filmmaker. If I can't do that, I've failed.

What was one of the biggest surprises from that first year?

That 3,000 people showed up. We just had street marketing. We actually had some ads and articles in the paper about it; it was sort of new and interesting. We actually had a lot of press, which probably helped. I was definitely surprised that anybody came, and I guess the highlight was that Jon Cryer who played Ducky in *Pretty in Pink* came. He had a film in the festival and he came; this was even before he was famous for that show. I had this memory of driving Ducky around in my $500 Datsun, taking him back from the festival. That was a highlight of the weekend for sure.

You've defined what failure is, so what is success?

Again, people in attendance. Now I'm not quite as worried about the money part; it's successful if I can pay off everything, and if I'm lucky have a little bit left over—that's what it used to be. Now, I have to have a good show, a good audience, a good turnout. They don't all have to like it, which has always been my policy; I used to proudly wear walk outs as a badge of pride, a sign of non-universal accessibility, and I thought that was great. We had more walkouts back then than we do now, which is currently barely ever. We viewed being able to annoy or offend as sort of a sign of success, so we used to play a lot more potentially offensive titles. It was the underground side of the independent film world we embraced back then. Today, though, success to me is a full house that starts on time with some good feedback from the audience to know they enjoyed the movie.

When did you go non-profit?

Going non-profit was kind of weird, because for the first few years, we were set up as a fiscally sponsored project of a group called Media Alliance. Then, I brought on someone to sell sponsorships. She didn't like the idea of having to give a cut of sponsorship money to this fiscal sponsor, so she went and took it upon herself to deal with the IRS and get our 501(c)(3) paperwork done. I wasn't really highly prioritizing it myself at the time, but anyway, that's how it happened, and I'm glad she did it.

Because we don't have a paid membership, and we don't really need to sell sponsorship to be successful, being a non-profit is not a huge deal for us. It's really helpful for certain things like getting product donations, which we could always use, but a lot of folks don't even ask about our non-profit status.

What was your original board like and how did you choose board members?

It's not structured like a typical nonprofit board. It was and continues to be a group of friends who are fans of the festival or people who I've handpicked to be on it —and they don't get to do very much. They get to come to the festival.

Since the founding, I've taken seminars and classes, and I've learned all about how organizations are supposed to use their board for resources and for fundraising, but I sort of feel like after doing this for going on 18 years I'm that dog that can't learn new tricks. I experiment with little things here and there, but having a bigger active board is just something I have no interest in pursuing at the moment.

Looking back, do you think it was necessary to become a 501(c)(3)? Do you think you would have had to, or do you think you would have stayed a for-profit?

It's hard to say. I think it depends on how complicated the process would have been. We did it in 2001, before you could just go online and download something on how to become a non-profit. But even with all the complications, I was working at a non-profit before I started the festival, and was able to see firsthand what benefits they were getting from that status. So, I think I probably still would have, since I always tried to copy the SF International Film Festival in my modest DIY punk rock way.

Do you go after grants?

Sort of. We have two grants from the city: The city's art fund, which we have received since the start of the festival, and the city's general fund, which is not quite so consistent, depending on the general funding, I suppose. These make up about twenty percent of our budget. Otherwise, we have applied for some other grants here and a couple academy ones and arts funders, but none of them have ever panned out and I never highly prioritize going after them and I don't currently have a staffer who is paid to do research and file grant applications for us, because it's never worked out in the past.

What is your budget?

The whole organization produces three film festivals and a bunch of one-off events throughout the year. The whole organization's budget is roughly around $200k, but it's been as high as $250k or as low as $160k, and then each individual festival is smaller. The February event, the oldest one, that budget is about $100k. The documentary festival, DocFest, is about $60k and then the genre festival, Another Hole in the Head, comes in at about $35k or so.

In the main festival, the independent, how many films did you show this year?

I think it was 75, which is an almost 50-50 of features and shorts, so 30-some features and 40-some shorts. DocFest has about 90 films, 40 features and 50 shorts. The genre festival, which usually runs two weeks, ends up being about 30 features and another 20 short films.

For the main festival, how big is your audience?

For SF IndieFest, 11,000 last year, and DocFest was about 7,000 and change, HoleHead about 4,000.

Each one is about a week, right?

Two weeks. DocFest and IndieFest are two weeks on two screens. We also did satellite screenings in the East Bay, but that stopped this year. We also are doing another week of screenings at another theater in the city, which is why the festival is going to be a bit bigger. It ends up being approximately 100 screening slots.

How many volunteers does it take?

I have a very small staff of volunteers, and I only use them for getting people in and out of the theater, checking tickets, doing quick sweeps, picking up popcorn bags and cups, stuff like that. I'm going to guess that the team is twenty, maybe thirty people.

Do you have paid staff for that time?

We have some, and they are very modestly compensated. We are probably the least well-paid festival in San Francisco, but we have a handful people we have to pay.

At what point did this become full time for you?

I was still working full time at the SF International Festival until 2000, and the first IndieFest was January 1999. After the second festival, I was no longer full time at the film society, but I did go back and work as their Operations Manager in 2001, in addition to working full-time and then some at the bar I'd just opened. Since 2003, though, I've just been dedicating most of my time to IndieFest, but I kind of feel like indie fest was always full time while also doing other things. I think starting in 2010 or '11, I started picking up some gigs in my off season. I've working at Burning Man since 2005 and I've worked at the Jewish Film Festival for a few of years in my off season, which is currently in the Summer/Fall.

How did your initial programing strategy change to the way you choose films now?

That's also hard to answer, because I stopped programming after year two or three. One of the first staff members I brought on was a programmer, because I hate rejecting films. This is especially true with documentaries, because I think almost every single documentary screener I see has an audience somewhere, no matter how big or small. I knew that there were people who just love the concept of programming and think it's the greatest job in the world, so finding people to do it has been pretty easy.

What I do instead is have people who understand what we're looking for, which is something unique and well-made, and then task them to bring that to the festival. I think our audiences were a lot more tolerant of poorly made films that we just liked than they are now. Nowadays they expect everything to be polished and perfect, so the programming side is still "show me something different, show me something weird, just something that stands out." The programmer guys really like mumble cores, and they'll do two or three mumble core films in every festival and I have to say that I don't know if we need that many films of people living in their loft in Brooklyn and talking about their life for an hour and a half each time. Anyway, that was what was happening until we started documenting in our programming.

I say "our," because while I wasn't dealing with it, I was bringing on people who I thought had the same idea about what we should be showing at the festival.

Talk about the festival today. What are some of your biggest challenges?

Funding is always hard, because marketing is the challenge that I feel like I spend most of my time on. There is so much stuff going on in San Francisco every week; you can't just count on "Oh, nothing else is going on Monday and Tuesday, so we'll definitely get people coming to this," because that's just not true. There are 500 things going on Monday and Tuesday, and we have to cut through the noise. We also don't go after corporate sponsors. I won't turn away sponsorship money if it's brought to me, but I don't have anybody out there looking for it.

Keeping staff consistently is hard, because it's so low paying. It's the kind of thing people can do on the side, but it still takes up time so it's hard to hold on to folks if they end up getting a "real" job. Also around here, due to the rising cost of living, a lot of people move, so I've lost a fair number of programmers to just that alone.

Those are the biggies, I suppose. Everybody wants to get paid more, and I don't mean just people necessarily, but also venues and other sorts of vendors we use. Costs rise but you can't really raise ticket prices so much to make up for it, so we're sort of in a bind with it being mostly funded by box office.

If you're not going after major corporate sponsors and most of your time is spent marketing, how are you reaching out to your audience to bring them to the shows?

We have a publicist who gets stories written in the papers and the blogs. We also do partnerships with event sites. These sites have a pretty large built-in audience, so word of mouth is great. We also have a very large audience that's developed after 18 years. They're sort of the ambassadors to the community, getting our emails and passing them around, which also helps us pick up new audiences.

Do you reward those influencers on your mailing list at all?

We put on a good show for them—that's the reward. No, we don't do anything special.

Since you're doing a lot of feature films, talk about some of the distributors.

Deals and distributors change with time too, of course. The industry has changed a lot in 18 years. We have distributors who reach out to us but never any big ones. We never had to worry "What will I do if Miramax wants me to show their latest piece of crap film; what would I tell them?" The distributors that we work with tend to be kind of small and often foreign, so it doesn't really change the game so much except that films tend to be more polished than the ones we consider from unsolicited submissions.

Then, of course, there's the screening fee situation. When distributors aren't involved there isn't a screening fee problem. That has changed a fair amount recently; we had to come up with policies. The solution came down to not showing very many films from distributors nowadays that have a high screening fee, which are almost always annoying to negotiate. We definitely have lost a few that we would have liked to have shown, but that's the main change I think with distributors. One distributor in Spain, Promofest, sends us a box of DVDs every IndieFest and DocFest of thirty feature films or something they wanted us to consider, very regional interest type stuff that we never really end up showing, and now they don't do that because they own that submission service. They just load them all up onto our ClickforFestivals site.

You have multiple sites like WAB and FilmFreeway and ClickForFest. How have filmmakers' expectations of film festivals over the years?

When we started way back when, before there were submission services, you would have to send out letters to people, and they would send you letters back with a VHS tape of their submission, or a request for an application form. You would then have to send them a photocopied piece of paper with all the stuff you wanted, and then send it back with a VHS tape and that's how you submitted to festivals. When the Internet service companies popped up to middleman that process, it was much easier for filmmakers to find out about the newer systems.

Anyway, we ended up with a lot more submissions. In terms of how the filmmakers changed, it has become less of a party than it was in the beginning and more commercial minded. Before the digital camera revolution it was very expensive to make a movie. Not that it's cheap now, but it's easier now than it was ten years ago and I think people spent a little bit more time crafting them. Now, there's just a lot more films. But I'm also not watching a lot of these submissions; I haven't wanted to pick the submissions in a long time, except for programming the animation programs because I just happen to like cartoons.

It's hard to say how filmmakers changed. It's definitely easier for people to find out more, but that's just a result of the internet more than anything else. I have no idea what's going on in the film schools, what they're teaching people and whether there are more students.

Over the years, what type of programs have you implemented that work beautifully, that have kept doing for a long time?

I think you're asking me about the ones I had fun with, which are our parties. To me they're sort of necessary for a film festival, to keep the festival festive. I used to be a club promoter, so of course I tend to gravitate towards all things that involve parties.

For a long time, we had a programmer named Bruce Fletcher who was really big into Japanese films, so we got to be known as a festival that showed a lot of really great, completely bizarre feature films from Japan, almost always on 35mm. I had all these bills from shipping films back and forth to Japan, which was killing me. We had two or three every festival for a good four or five years running, I think. That was actually really great; we built an audience in San Francisco for those movies and I think that was a wonderful thing to have done. When Bruce left , the new programmer who took over his role had a much broader focus than he did, so we didn't do as many Japanese films but definitely better, more crazy films from all over the world, so I'm definitely happy with that change.

I have this annual Big Lebowski party, I think this year will be the twelfth or thirteenth year doing it. People come every year for that.

What are some programs you implemented that have not been so successful or that you had to kill?

I was trying to do screenings in the East Bay, which I've been unable to crack for a very long time. I tried a bunch of different venues and different ways of doing it: regular theaters, then black box folding-chair theaters, all kinds of different ones. We never figured out how to reach the audience in Berkley so that was always very frustrating, so I have basically given up. It's a shame because a lot of the people who used to be the whacky artist types in San

Francisco now live in the East Bay. While we were showing films in the East Bay, we would do a show of hands in the San Francisco theater and ask who here is from the East Bay and half the audience would raise their hands. You guys do know we're showing movies in Berkeley right now, right? They just didn't go to see movies over there; it was really frustrating. That's the biggest one that I gave up on.

How many years did you try that?

I think over a decade for both IndieFest and DocFest. We never bothered with Another Hole in the Head. Most festivals I would try to do something over there and most of the time it just didn't work. I thought the documentary one would be great there, but we couldn't even get people out to that. When it's not working I don't want to give up, but I don't want to keep losing money. Then you do stuff cheaper and you lose even more people, because people aren't used to going to folding chair auditoriums. I've learned that from DocFest, where it started with a budget that was hardly anything, $2,500 or something.

In the first year we showed movies in what had been a church that the Academy of Art had just bought, and they let us use it for free. The second year, I showed movies in my friend's night club that he had not quite finished opening; it didn't have a liquor license yet so he was trying to find any way to get money in there. We screened there, and then for years three, four, five and six, I put out folding chairs in an auditorium in the Mission and did a screening there, but the following year, I thought it was big enough to move to an expensive theater that I had to rent for real money. The audience doubled that year just from me going from an auditorium with folding chairs to a legitimate movie house. That was a really powerful thing to learn. I thought people would just go to wherever I took the shows; if they want to see documentaries, they'll go. Turns out yes, some of them will do that, the hardcore ones, but if you're dealing with casual moviegoers, which is most of the people who come to your festival, they like to be in a real theater. You'd think it would be obvious, but it was not obvious to me at the time.

What, if anything would you have changed from the start?

I don't know. If I had been a little less of a DIY punk rock kid and a little bit more business minded, I think the festival would not have been such a struggle. It would have been a different kind of struggle maybe, but I think if I had actually known something about business and thought about having an active board, having someone from the get-go who was interested and able to sell sponsorships, that would have shored up the finances. It would not have been so paperclip and duct taped together, but again, I really am an '80s punk kid.

I haven't really changed, so I'm really glad the organization is kind of the same way. It would have been weird to try to do it differently. I do look at organizations younger than mine… stronger, healthier, doing fabulous things, and looking great, and I envy their ability to do the business part better, because by doing so, they put on a better show. The audiences appreciate it, the town appreciates it, so that's one thing I guess I would do differently; but, knowing who I am, I'm not sure it's possible to have done it any other way.

You've been there from the start. Do you see an exit strategy at some point? Do you think you'll be doing this forever?

I think about that all the time. There was a time, a decade ago or maybe longer, when I thought every year would be my last. I thought, "This is ridiculous. Why am I still doing this?" Then every year I couldn't think of anything else to do, so I'd just do it again, just to keep it going. Basically I was really discontented with the whole business. I wasn't having fun anymore, just doing the same thing all the time, and it was such a drag. That's basically how I ended up starting these other festivals, DocFest and Hole in the Head, because I wanted another project.

That's actually how I stay interested in doing it now. I can't imagine doing this ten years from now, but I didn't think that ten years ago either, that's for sure. I haven't come up with what I would do next. I've been working for myself for so long that for while I was afraid I wasn't going to be able to work in an office if I ever had to again. That's why I took these seasonal jobs, just to make sure I could in fact go in, sit at a desk and do what someone told me I needed to do. Apparently I haven't completely lost that skill.

I thought maybe if a company that I really like, say Alamo Drafthouse, had a place for me, then maybe I would leave IndieFest and go to work for them, just because I really like what they do. I have to say I definitely liked when I worked at the SF Film Society, I really enjoyed going to work every day. There was not a single morning I didn't get up happy to be going to work. I even liked the staff meetings, because I just loved hearing what other people in the office were doing on this project. If I found a place that I thought was going to give me that experience, maybe I would quit doing IndieFest and do that.

I considered handing IndieFest off to somebody else and just overseeing it, but it's hard, it's sort of your baby. I birthed this thing and I've been taking care of it for 18 years and it's going to be hard to end it or pass it on. I fantasize about living abroad, but then, instead of thinking about what would I do there for a job, I think about whether i could do this job from there and then why I would ever do any different job when I can keep doing this job. But it's hard to imagine doing it again; it's hard to imagine doing it ten to twenty years from now, especially when I remember I'm 45 years old and no longer my own target demographic.

My audience is people who are in their 20s or 30s, before they grow up and have children. Once you grow up and have children, you're not going to go out to the movies much just in general, let alone buying a pass to watch a whole bunch of movies over doing anything else. When you're not your own demographic should you still be doing this? Most of my programmers are 30-somethings, and I really should think about an exit strategy, but I haven't figured it out.

Where do you see the event in three to five years?

I see it the same as it is today. It's sort of sad to say. One of the good things about working a non-profit or your own business is that you don't have to live by this constant growth idea that businesses seem to emphasize. Not that I know much about business, but just from reading the paper and seeing press releases when I was at the International Film Festival, they seem to constantly be obsessed with showing growth, but I don't actually feel like I have to show growth. If we lose audience numbers because they hate things about the festival and they move away, we replace them. It's not a huge stress, and I actually don't have a problem with it being more or less the same festival today as it will be three years from now.

What are you most proud of? What do you think has given the event the biggest stamp of Jeff Ross? Say you weren't with it tomorrow, what do you think would say, "I was here"?

Well, the fact that it actually happens every year. My business card says "doer of things", and that's what I'm most proud of: that I actually end up doing the things I say I'm going to do and people show up.

Aside from that, the most "Jeff Ross" part of it is probably the lack of corporate involvement, the lack of stuff that we don't do as opposed to the stuff that we do. It's still really grass roots and DIY, and I'm most proud of that. I'm proud that we're able to do this stuff—"we" being "me"—in a way that doesn't make me uncomfortable. We still pull it off without pissing off too many people, though pissing off a few people is just inevitable. I'm proud of being able to pull it off with a finite amount of resources.

One of the best experiences involved one of the two grants we applied for from the city. They have a public hearing, so you can go down, sit in the audience and listen to the granting staff, and you can hear them talking about your application. You can't interact with them while people listen to the discussion. One of the best moments was probably one guy looking at our DocFest application and he just couldn't believe how much we were doing for so little. We have a 60 thousand dollar budget and yet we produce a relatively nice program guide, show a lot of films over a lot of days, have a lot of press coverage and all this impact. He couldn't believe it. I thought that was one of the nicest things anyone has said about me.

What challenges do you see for the future of film festivals?

I haven't checked in certain cities, but there's a fair amount of cannibalizing, there's a lot of people doing new ones all the time and trying to make a mark. In San Francisco they used to say there were forty film festivals, and I don't know if that actually is true, but there are definitely a lot. I worry about the organizers who lose the idea of a film festival where you put on a show, and instead you have a little two-hour shorts program and you call it a film festival. That's hurting my moniker, my brand.

Then, of course, there's the internet festival screenings. Having a festival shown through the internet. I don't feel like that's… It's certainly not what I do. I understand why some people do it, or the whole "augment their brick-and-mortar festival with an online presence," but it just isn't part of what I'm interested in. I don't want to contribute to a culture where people aren't going to movies as much anymore because they can just watch movies at home. The festival still has value as a curating tool and, to me, my whole purpose in life is to bring people together for shared experiences, and that continues to be a challenge. They say that the movie going has gone down except for blockbusters. *Mad Max* comes out and that's an "event"; everybody has to take part in the event. That movie sells tons of tickets whereas the latest stoner comedy doesn't sell as many tickets, because people thought, "I'll just watch that when it comes out on Netflix."

I feel like we have to address that by just being an event all the time. Every show is an event. And from what I understand from people who work in the industry here, we're doing okay with our audiences. People are coming out to the festivals because it's a special event, even though they could make a list of all those films that we curate and then wait for them to pop up on their streaming service of choice. That might change in the future, too. Who knows? A film festival might just end up being a list of the best downloads that I could find on bit torrent and you should watch.

What words of wisdom would you have for someone wanting to start a film festival?

I think the first one is to decide what type of film festival you want to have. There are at least two kinds of film festivals. One is interested in championing films and filmmakers. They often market themselves as being filmmaker friendly; basically they're the ones who want to get your film as much exposure as possible on the internet, in the press, that sort of thing. They're interested in making discoveries about films and finding new filmmakers to champion, being able to say they knew them before they were huge. That I think is one focus.

The type that I do, is audience-focused. I'm more interested in the show and getting a group of people together for shared experiences. Part of that is having a filmmaker there, sure, but not because I feel like I need to provide something to the filmmaker, but because the audience appreciates talking to the filmmaker. I don't even like horror films and sci-fi films, but I started a horror and sci-fi festival because I knew that there were people who did. I'm not interested in necessarily championing those films, but I am interested in entertaining people who would like to see them. That's the first step, what kind of festival are you planning to have? Do you want to put on a show for people in your town, or do you want to make discoveries about films?

The second issue is how much free stuff you can get and how much stuff you can get for very little money, because unless you have a lot of money to burn the first couple of years, you're going to have to get as much free stuff as possible. That's probably the same for someone who is making a movie. I'm told this is how you make a movie, you make a list of all the stuff you can get for free and those are the things you have to use to make a movie. In this case it's venues, advertising, staff and resources. How much of that can you get for nothing or very little? You start from there. I don't believe young film festivals should charge for their call for entries, because they haven't earned it yet. I believe they have to put on the festival and prove that they can actually deliver people to screenings before they can ask for somebody to give as operating revenue just to consider their film. What's important is, "Who's your audience and what kind of event are you trying to put on?"

LISA VANDEVER
CineKink

Co-founder and director of CineKink, Lisa Vandever oversees and curates the organization's annual film festival and touring series, now in its twelfth season. A producer and consultant with over twenty years of experience in film and television, Vandever was formerly the director of programming for a regional network of public television stations, worked as a development executive for two New York-based independent production companies, and was associate producer of the Sundance award-winning feature film, Songcatcher.

In addition to serving on the board of directors of the National Coalition for Sexual Freedom, she also volunteered on its media committee, alerting community members to media presentations of alternative sexuality, and encouraging feedback. She has spoken several times on the intersection of film and sexuality at the prestigious SXSW conference, with additional appearances including the International Film Festival Summit, Film Festival Academy, DIY Convention, Sex 2.0, MomentumCon, CatyalystCon and Leather Leadership Conference.

What was your background before you started CineKink?

My background is film and television, and I have my MFA in film. I moved to New York to get a film job and was working in film development, and just really stumbled into doing festivals. That's sort of the fun thing about how it happened. Someone said "hey, let's start a film festival." And we did! Whereas in film development, you make notes on a project forever and something might not ever happen.

Tell us about the origination story. How did it come to be?

CineKink is very niche-y. I'd actually done a festival before it that was even more specific. It was the New York S/M Film Festival, when I first moved to New York. I had fallen in with the S/M scene through an organization called The Eulenspiegel Society—and it was a whole new world to me. The group wanted to do a screening series as outreach to bring new people in, and they were going to rent films from Blockbuster and charge admission to attend. I suggested they approach things a little more professionally. (That's a pet peeve of mine, and I see it all the time. People have no clue about licensing and copyright issues. They think they can just screen a film for a group with no problem.)

So the guy who had the idea in the first place and I became co-founders of that festival. We had a lot of fun producing the event, but the organization had a fairly meddlesome board that seemed to want control over everything. After dealing with that for three years, and discovering I really loved what I was doing, combining my interests in sex and film, I decided to keep running some kind of festival. I came up with the name CineKink, secured the web domain, and persuaded the previous festival's co-founder, Michael, to go in with me.

What was the original mission?

CineKink was set up to celebrate and explore sexuality, and to promote sex-positive and kink-friendly media. Part of that mission came out of my volunteer work for the National Coalition of Sexual Freedom, where I was helping put out alerts for negative portrayals in the media. I thought it would be nice to also give props to positive works.

You had one group in mind when you started. Did you have a bigger audience in mind as it grew?

Our original audience consisted of The Eulenspiegel Society members, their friends, and a few people who heard about the event. We also had a large audience of press. We sent out a bunch of releases, and they were like, "Oh, we never even thought about S/M in movies." When they showed interest—and wrote about the event, that's when it created interest to a larger, outside audience. And as we increased the scope of our programming to include other aspects of sexuality, we also started doing outreach to groups whose interests might overlap.

How long did it take you to create the first festival?

We already had a template from the first festival. Going back over the years, it's shifted a little, but the original template is still there. The toughest part has been finding the venues and the films. The first battle was finding a theater that would welcome us, and even in New York, with a sexuality-focused festival, that was a tough sell.

So a year, three months, six months?

Thinking back to the first one, I guess it took about six months to put together the first festival, maybe less than that.

How did you differentiate the S/M festival from CineKink?

CineKink expanded our focus beyond just S/M to embrace a wider range of sexuality. Initially, with the S/M festival, we found films through distributors, and tracking down films that had been in theaters. Going into CineKink is when we began bringing in independent films, reaching out to filmmakers with a call for entries.

The first year of CineKink, what was your greatest fear?

Losing all of our money —the festival was totally bootstrapped. I can remember counting the proceeds one evening, and Michael and I were very nervous. We came out of that first year with a slight loss. I also lost Michael as a partner in the festival, albeit amicably. He thought this was going to be a lot easier going in, but decided it was not for him…so I bought him out as a partner in CineKink.

What were some of the surprise successes that year?

How great it is when you find a film that enlivens the crowd, and they have that sense of discovery. Particularly for an audience that isn't used to seeing themselves portrayed positively on screen, it's incredibly electric to experience that with a like-minded set of folk.

The Eulenspiegel Society was a non-profit. When you set-up CineKink, did you set-up as non-profit as well?

No, CineKink is for-profit, though it perhaps hasn't always felt so. However, in terms of corporate structure we're an LLC.

What is the rationale behind that?

Before getting into film, I had worked in public television and had a lot of experience working with non-profit boards, and I really wanted to avoid that world and its complications if I could. I also have a number of friends who work for non-profits, and they advised me that because of the subject matter, our focus on sexuality, we'd probably be out of the running for most grants. The extra expense of putting together a non-profit entity wouldn't be worth it.

Being a for-profit entity, have you found it difficult to get sponsorships?

> Not in that sense, because we present sponsorships as a marketing opportunity. I think our biggest problem is the sexuality aspect. We have not been able to find mainstream sponsors, who are scared off by the potential controversy. And even within the sex industry, they haven't quite embraced the concept of sponsorship. I feel that recognition is afforded far too easily, and the worth of a sponsorship is often devalued.

So, tell me about the most current festival: the vital statistics.

> CineKink is six days. We start with a kick-off party on Tuesday, movies run through Saturday, and on Sunday night we present our awards, and an afterglow party. Last year, we showed 35 features and shorts in 14 programs.

How did you decide on the original program strategy?

> It was trial and error. We came in knowing we wanted a couple of very strong, proven features, while bringing in new works, which tended to be shorts. The selection process has evolved over the years, so now it's more about submitted works and, in many cases, we're premiering features. In the beginning, the festival was heavily curated, with works found by going to other festivals and by checking out their programs.

You said mainstream sponsors have been a hard nut to crack, and sex sponsors don't get it. What are some things you do to develop those relationships to try and explain to them how your niche works?

> We try to seek out the sex-positive businesses, for example, sex toy vendors that might enjoy the types of films we show, or who understand the educational component, or whose aesthetic matches ours. People are starting to get it, and understand that we're going after the same market—largely people who are smart, curious about sex, and want to explore.

> Lately, I've had a lot of philosophical thoughts about this. I worry that our audience thinks we take in a lot of sponsorship money, so they're perhaps less likely to support us. So I'm considering a move towards a membership base and soliciting individual donors.

Do you think it's because your potential sponsors see a ton of logos on your website and assume you're well funded?

Yes. In hindsight it's probably better to call them "partners" and not "sponsors."

Because organizations often receive in-kind donations instead of cash, so it's hard to determine who gave what, when all a potential sponsor sees are logos on your website. They might see Avis and think you received $20,000, when all you got was a week of free car rental.

Exactly. Or a stainless steel dildo for our auction.

How do you develop your relationship with distributors? Do you still work with them?

A little bit. We don't screen very many of the more widely-released kink movies anymore, unless it's a film we really want and have been tracking. Otherwise, we present such a focused, curated program, and have such a prominent position within our niche, it's become a real distinction for filmmakers to screen with us, and especially, to be a CineKink award winner.

Do you think some distributors are afraid to be pegged as a sex festival?

Yes, we've run into that. There was a documentary that came out a couple of years ago about swinging, which would have been perfect for us, and I kept getting the runaround from distributors. Then about a year later, the filmmakers were calling me back saying they'd made a mistake, and apologized. They were trying to build up their DVD sales. If they were at CineKink from the get-go, we'd have been pushing them all along.

What do you think are some of the biggest challenges facing your festival?

The main thing I'm facing right now is how to grow. Is it scalable? I'd like to see it became bigger, and be able to take a salary and hire some staff

At what point did CineKink become full-time for you?

It's only become full-time in combination with my family, with the past couple of years involving a lot of time traveling to be with my aging parents on the opposite coast. I've let go of some other freelance endeavors in the interim, but it's been so great to have CineKink to keep me centered. I feel like I have something I'm focused on and not just letting go of all my film stuff. It became a full focus probably about four years in, and when the touring started, the time commitment also expanded.

Talk about your touring program because I think that's a goal of a lot of festivals. Many can't seem to make the leap.

I don't know how you'd do a touring program without having a specific niche. Our tour got its start when an arts organization in San Francisco got in touch and asked us to present a CineKink screening. With that, we started looking at other cities. We started out trying to replicate a mini, two-day, on-the-road festival in different places, but it was too difficult to manage. It's been scaled back in most places to a "Best of CineKink" shorts-only program. People love shorts, as you know.

So you're repackaging the shorts screened in New York—shorts for other groups. Do you partner with existing organizations or events, or are you creating a screening from scratch?

It depends from city to city. In Chicago, we screen at the Leather Archives, and obviously they're pretty central in the S/M community there. But in other cities we might screen with an independent arthouse, then reach out to local, sex-positive groups and businesses to find our audience.

Talk about media relations, I assume for major outlets it's too hot to handle. How do you get marketing and media?

Actually outside of New York it's much easier, which you wouldn't think. There's so much going on in New York, it can be hard to get attention, but on the road, just packaging it as slightly titillating, we've had some great coverage. It's often just sending out a press release that we'll be in town, and then following up with a screener if there's interest.

Since you handle promotion all by yourself, do you think you've been effective?

We're caught between worlds—the adult entertainment world and mainstream world—and need to promote to both of them. We've had some past success bringing in a publicist to help build our presence in the adult world. Now, I'd like to see more visibility for us in the mainstream press, particularly publications targeted at a female audience. It's really about developing those relationships. I think I've done a pretty good job, and I will continue to work at it, but would really like to expand our reach.

Over the years, have you developed a program that just didn't meet your expectations?

Sunday matinees just didn't work for us. We tried those early on, thinking it would be a nice, cozy experience, but the time was all wrong for our audience. We've also found we don't usually do very well if we focus only on a gay-male audience for a program. I think that's because they have other, established outlets that offer works targeted at them.

What type of evaluations do you do after events? I mean you're a team of one, do you write out a post-event report for yourself? Do you take notes and review?

We have an amazing team of core volunteers who come out every year, always in the nick of time, and I rely on them for feedback on the event. I'd like to be more contemplative and really get a handle on what worked and what didn't—and always intend to do a post-event debriefing. Usually after the festival, though, we're so exhausted, and I don't have time to reflect. And then suddenly we're ramping up for the next year.

How do you define success? It does not necessarily have to be in the context of CineKink.

For me, it's happiness. I know it's superficial sounding, but if you can have balance in your life, it's all good. I feel like I'm doing something that matters, and the balance to that is I have a partner who makes a decent living, and who understands the mission of the festival, which allows me to do what I love. A bit more financial padding would be nice, but to be able to focus on CineKink is a real gift.

I'd say you're relatively active with the community of other festival directors. I know if I post something on the Film Festival Organizers Facebook group, you're going to respond. Talk about that resource and what you get out of a community of festival directors.

It's exactly what I wanted when I was starting out and it was just not available at the time. Particularly when you're starting out, you want to be able to ask others how much they charge, how much someone pays for something, if it's okay to do something a certain way, is it normal? A place to go to get that perspective and people who understand what you're going through is unique.

I agree. There's hundreds, if not thousands of festivals, all run very differently and by passionate people who want to make a difference. It's interesting they all have the same issues, but how they each tackle those issues is greatly different.

It's such a huge range. As a very small festival, when we're discussing budgets, some of the numbers are so out of the realm of anything I could imagine. It's the same thing I encountered when I worked at a small-market PBS station. I remember I was hanging out at the national PBS conference one year. We went into the Hospitality Suite and I was overwhelmed by the amount of swag in there: the amount of money spent on schmoozing would've been really better spent on programming. At the same time, though, there are so many commonalities, despite differences of scale or budget.

You've already touched on this: where you see the event in a few years? Since you're a one-woman shop, do you see an exit strategy for yourself in the future? Do you see it growing to the point where you can get out or do you see this as something you'll do indefinitely?

I'm committed to CineKink as long as it gives back that feeling of accomplishment and community. I do want to grow it so I can bring in other people, and start passing on more responsibilities. I don't know if I'd ever sell it, if I'd trust someone with my baby.

Looking back, is there anything you would have changed?

I think I would have tried to emphasize promotions and advertising more, and earlier. Maybe taken it a bit more seriously and pushed it a bit harder.

What are you most proud of—what DNA have you put into the event that you hope will have the biggest impact?

Creating an outlet that didn't exist before, one that has spurred a whole film movement. People who might not have even thought of making sexuality a focus of their films are now creating works with CineKink specifically in mind. Also, I am proud of creating sex-positive awareness, and growing a community of filmmakers.

How do you feel about upstarts and competitors?

Mixed. It really depends on how another festival views itself and its relationship with the community. Is it better to collaborate or to compete? One large festival, the Berlin Pornfilm Festival, along with a couple of others, has been great to partner with over the years, sharing suggestions on films and programs. Then, you'll see others events rise up, and then die down pretty rapidly. The new New York Porn Festival irked me a bit last year, coming out of nowhere and scheduled for the same dates as CineKink. That was definitely a big conflict, at least at first.

Are they showing more porn and you're showing more sex-positive films?

Well, the weird thing is they didn't really show that much more porn. Their program seemed more varied than that, a mix of genres like we do, but they used the porn name. Over the years, I've had a lot of angst about whether or not I wanted the word "porn" in our title because most of our programming isn't porn. And because people become so fixated with the very word.

In any case, eventually I talked to their founder. Looking at our Facebook friends, we only overlapped by two friends, meaning we're each reaching two very different crowds. Rather than fight for the same audience, it's far better to support one another and grow the audience as a whole. Raise everyone's boat, is the principle. It turned out they had a great first festival, and we had the best turnout we've ever experienced.

That's a good way to go about it, because you could probably have six sex-positive festivals and you probably wouldn't have the same audience because of distance, timing or film titles.

What challenges do you see for the future of the film festival industry?

Getting people out of the house. We need to define what our festivals are really all about, reinforce that sense of community and emphasize why they need to get off the sofa and into a theater seat.

One final question: What words of wisdom do you have for anyone wanting to start a film festival?

Know what you're getting into: research your dates, look for similar events and understand it's a lot of work. But also know how fun it is!

Are you glad you made the decision to do it?

Oh yeah. I don't know what else I'd be doing. It's the perfect thing for me!

NINA GILDEN SEAVEY
SILVERDOCS (now AFI Docs)

Nina Gilden Seavey is an Emmy Award-winning filmmaker and nearly 30-year veteran of the documentary world. Her work can be seen in cinemas, on television, on multiple platforms in ancillary and digital media, and in museum installations across the globe. Seavey is the director of The Documentary Center in the School of Media and Public Affairs at The George Washington University in Washington, DC, which she founded in 1990. She concurrently serves as Co-Director of the Center for Innovative Media at GWU. In 2012, Seavey was named one of the top fifty journalism professors in the U.S. by journalismdegree.org. She holds the academic rank of Full Research Professor of History and Media and Public Affairs. In 2002, Seavey became the Founding Director of the Silverdocs: AFI-Discovery Documentary Festival (now AFI DOCS). She continued with the festival as Executive Producer, Programmer, and senior member of the management team from 2003 to 2008.

What was your background before you started Silverdocs? Was the transition to a festival seamless?

I've always have been, first and foremost, a filmmaker. At the time I launched Silverdocs, I'd been a filmmaker for over ten years and had been the director of The Documentary Center for most all of that time. I'd always had a toe in the festival world, but with no formal connection or experience other than attending events in which my films were screening. As a filmmaker with a growing family, I was always very selective about how much time I spent away from home, so I was certainly not considered a "regular" on the festival circuit by any means.

What I did have, however, were very solid and long-term relationships with both the American Film Institute in Washington, DC and with Discovery Communications. I had been running a program with AFI called "Artists on Film" and in which actors and directors such as Sissy Spacek and Norman Jewison came to George Washington University, we hosted a symposium, and then screened a retrospective of their work at the AFI Theater, which was located at the time at the Kennedy Center. In addition, I had made, with my then-partner Paul Wagner, one of Discovery Channel's first large commissioned documentary films, *The Battle of the Alamo*. So while I wasn't one of the "usual suspects" on the festival circuit, I did have close relationships with both founding organizations and that's where the roots of my relationship with Silverdocs began.

In 1998, Ray Barry [Director, AFI Silver Theatre] came to me with the news that AFI would be moving from the Kennedy Center to Silver Spring, Maryland at the same time that Discovery Networks would also be relocating its world headquarters just down the street from what would become the newly-renovated AFI Silver Theatre. Both institutions were trying to find a way to celebrate their new proximity in the designated Silver Spring Arts and Entertainment District and decided that a documentary festival might be just the right public statement about their shared common commitment to non-fiction filmmaking. While AFI, as an institution, had always had a general interest in documentaries, it was by no means a focus of their work either in exhibition or at the Conservatory. Therefore, Ray asked if I would come on as a consultant to help create a sketch of what a new documentary festival in the nation's capital might look like.

As events unfolded, that event would not take place until 2003, but work on it began, in earnest, before the new millennium. I communicated back and forth with AFI in both DC and Los Angeles in defining their vision for documentaries, wrote reports, surveyed the then-current festival world, and carved out a prospectus for "something new" in what was already a crowded festival calendar.

AFI at that time was led by Jean Picker Firstenberg. She was always a real class and obviously had deep ties in Hollywood—but equally strong ones in Washington, DC. She had family in the area and the spirit of the legislation signed by President Johnson that created the American Film Institute was central to her approach to her role as CEO. For me, having been a Washingtonian for more than two decades, I believed that this new event should represent the unique opportunities of the city's geography, its place on the world stage, and yet still emphasize its vibrant, diverse, and frequently eclectic local community (which many from outside DC don't even know exists). Washington is frequently a city full of contradictions and we all felt this new festival needed to embrace the multi-varied facets of what the city embodies.

Given my lack of direct involvement in the festival world in the late '90's, one of my first recommendations was that they hire a "real" film festival director—somebody who was truly involved in an established festival and who had already run a major exhibition program. AFI and Discovery did just that, but as delays upon delays postponed the opening of AFI Silver Theatre—a large, complicated, restoration of an old 1936 movie palace—that initial person moved on. Another qualified person was then similarly hired, who then ultimately fell prey to the same unfortunate outcome as months of waiting and planning stretched into years. During this entire time, I remained a confidant and general adviser to the festival (and their directors), a kind of "ambassador without portfolio."

By 2002, we were moving perilously close to the opening of the theatre, set for April of 2003, and the launch of the festival two months later. It was a very chaotic time—the theatre itself was still unfinished and huge portions of Silver Spring were under construction. The next thing you know, it was October of 2002 and the festival still didn't have a director for the inauguration of this new (very well financed, thanks to Discovery) festival. So AFI and Discovery again asked me to take the helm. I was hesitant both because of my limited experience at festivals, and because I already had a full-time job as the Director of the Documentary Center with a full cohort of graduate students ready to enter my annual Institute for Documentary Filmmaking in January 2003. Now up against a wall, Murray Horwitz, who had just signed on as the CEO of the AFI Silver, called Stephen Joel Trachtenberg, GW's President, and asked if I could be released for the next eight months. GW agreed, we figured out a deal, and I went to work for AFI. As for my hesitancy about not being a "festival person," my wonderful colleague, Christian Gaines, who was head of AFI Festivals in Los Angeles gave me wise words of advice. He said, "Nina, just make sure every night you show a movie and throw a party and you'll be fine!" Obviously it was much more complicated than that but when you boil it down to its barest skeleton, that is what festivals do.

So, I became the Founding Director of Silverdocs until they could find a replacement for me the following year. But as it happened, that first year was so successful I was asked to stay on for another six years as the Executive Producer of the festival, allowing me to split my time between GW and AFI.

So from initial idea to the first event was four years? That seems like a very long gestation.

It was. But it was necessary—and timed with the opening of the new theatre, the renaissance of downtown Silver Spring, and the opening of the headquarters of two large media enterprises. So it was a lot of moving parts.

In that time, you went through quite a few festival directors. What were some of these staffing or leadership issues?

This was a very particular case. Not only were we trying to launch a major event on the festival calendar, but here were two very large institutions trying to figure out how they could make a marriage. AFI was boosting their relatively small presence in the Washington, DC area with the opening of the AFI Silver Theatre. It was a hallmark event both culturally and for the local community, with the support of Montgomery County and other public and private monies raised for the major investment in the reconstruction and the on-going maintenance of the facility. On the other side of the street, Discovery was opening a brand new world headquarters with over 2,000 employees. So you had these two very different institutions colliding. Who was going to be able to manage that relationship—and how was it going to be managed? Who was going to navigate the various competing interests between a non-profit arts organization and a commercial business enterprise? How were we going to ensure that all of the various perspectives were understood and responded to—from the AFI, to Discovery, to the Washington DC area writ large, to the film festival stalwarts, and to the local community who now had a big stake in the game? It was definitely not a typical film festival genesis.

But I had a lot of experience in management—and I am a very political person. I worked in the Carter Administration, on Capitol Hill, and I've also worked for a number of presidential candidates. I knew politics, I'd worked for large media outlets as a journalist and then, obviously, had been a long-time filmmaker and an active member of a major university. I have a range of assets that I think are not necessarily valued in the festival world, because one doesn't often don't need these particular constellation of skills in a more traditional festival setting. Well, in this situation, one needed to know a lot about business, commercial enterprises, politics, and the movement of large public and private institutions—and then, of course, there was the whole regular array of activities in actually creating and managing a film festival.

Did the event have a mission from the start? And since this was such a long planning period, as you were developing the event over the years, did you change or modify your mission?

I think initially there was a very big question about whether the festival should be more TV oriented or more oriented to independent film. Discovery, a television cable company, had an obvious interest in television documentaries. AFI had an interest in the bourgeoning independent documentary community. So even in the late 1990's, there was initially this idea we would show, for example, traditional science and natural history documentaries, and that would make the event feel much more like a television showcase than a filmic one.

As the festival evolved, we jettisoned that vision because that idea couldn't live in the festival world and still have credibility. Why would the film industry and audiences want to see documentaries in a movie theater that they could turn on their televisions and see it the next day? To their credit, I think Discovery came to understand a world in which they didn't participate. In their own evolution over the years they did dabble in theatrically-driven films with Alex Gibney, Werner Herzog, and others, but those never felt like a good match for the company and indeed they ultimately faded away from the company's programming slate. But at the launch of Silverdocs, the world of the theatrical documentary was still far from Discovery's aesthetic. And yet the company, as represented by Senior Executive Vice President Don Baer, came to appreciate that in order for the event to have credibility with the press, the industry and with filmmakers that their core business would support one form of documentary programming but their substantial contribution to the festival—which was north of $1 million per year at the time—would support the exhibition of an entirely different kind of work.

To ensure the autonomy of the festival, and to maintain its credibility, we erected a very strong firewall between Silverdocs's programming department and Discovery so we could legitimately say that this was not a "Discovery Channel Promotional Event" but in fact a legitimate independently-programmed film festival. That was an incredibly important statement for us to make. As most documentaries then (and now) were supported by television entities, why would an HBO or a PBS allow one of their films to be screened in a festival that was being programmed, headlined, and marketed as "their brand" by a competitor? Still, some networks had a good bit of discomfort with the AFI-Discovery partnership because never before had a broadcaster or cable-caster in the documentary industry also been a purveyor of a festival under whose banner competing companies would show their work. In thinking about it now, I must admit it was a bit of a stretch, but most companies, PBS in particular, came across the threshold quite nicely and actually became a Founding Sponsor of The Silverdocs Industry Conference.

So, there was a lot of groping around at the beginning as to how this would all work with people sometimes colliding together as we figured it out. Finally I simply decided that Mary Kerr, who was our new Director of Programming, would not be allowed to go across the street to meet with the people at Discovery until she locked the program. And Discovery, to their credit, supported this notion of independence in order to allow us to gain our footing and move towards legitimacy in a circumstance that was, up until that point, pretty uncharted territory.

As you were building the event, did you have an audience in mind?

In preparation for this chat, I went back over our 2003 wrap report, and it made me realize, in some ways, how limited our aspirations were for the first year. I mean, first of all, we were nobodies in the independent documentary film industry. As evidence of this, people from throughout the industry were constantly challenging me as to why we needed yet another documentary festival. We already had Full Frame, Big Sky was launching around that time, and Sundance, obviously, programmed the best documentaries. Everybody questioned the very need for the event and, worse, wondered whether this was just another show for Discovery. It was all pretty disheartening.

So one problem was, "will the industry show up?" That seemed extremely doubtful—there was already too much industry suspicion towards the festival. Plus, there was this whole other part of it which was that Silver Spring itself, where people had to come to see these films, was literally a construction zone, with much of it in ruins. Much of the city was either boarded up because businesses had fled, or because there was a tremendous amount of construction. You have to remember that the move of both Discovery and AFI to Silver Spring was part of the creation of an "Arts and Entertainment District" that would (hopefully) be the anchors to a renaissance to the community that several decades before had been a thriving business and residential center but which was now quite dilapidated and downtrodden.

Worse, no one had ever heard of Silver Spring and kept referring to as "Silver Springs" which made our local community crazy. And it was so non-descript anyway—it wasn't in DC proper and people from outside of Washington had no geographic context for why a festival would be in such a place.

So Silver Spring was a mess. Other than the new Discovery headquarters, there was no place to hold a party. So we erected tents in what is now the Silver Spring Triangle. I made the contractor put up big signs because I didn't want people falling into holes—I mean it was dangerous. When I started working in the theater, we had to wear hardhats because everything (including the theatre) was still under construction and it was all so desolate that we had to be escorted to our cars at the end of the evening because it wasn't safe to walk alone.

The industry, the press, even people from neighboring communities had no end of questions: Where was this place? Where were people going to park? Was it safe? Why should I contemplate going there for entertainment? People from every vantage point simply didn't trust the whole notion of a film festival in Silver Spring. But I actually (naively?) believed that we could bring the community together in a moment of celebration that only documentary film can create.

So how do you overcome all this skepticism? I thought, "Everybody loves sports." So we built an entire strand around sports films—films that audiences could come and enjoy and maybe even walk away with a smile on their faces. We celebrated the strand with a night of football on the big screen called *Tight on the Spiral* featuring Steve Sabol, President of NFL Films, in conversation with Pulitzer Prize-winning journalist David Maraniss, who had recently published *When Pride Still Mattered: A Life of Vince Lombardy*. Some of the biggest documentaries ever have been sports documentaries and NFL Films was a true pioneer in the art of cinematography and storytelling in that genre. That evening was a big surprise for everyone who was in attendance. Indeed, in her review, a reporter from Indiewire said while she hated the idea of a football, she had to admit that it was the best night of film she'd seen all year.

And of course, we screened more traditional festival fare addressing politics, social issues, and culture. We programmed some very prominent films such as My Architect, which was a very big film at the time.

That was also the year that my mentor, Charles Guggenheim, died. In his honor, I created the Guggenheim Symposium. I took the last recorded interview with Charles that had been done by David McCullough shortly prior to his death and integrated that into a panel and screening that became a true celebration of his life. It was a very profound and moving night and has continued to be an ongoing homage to my late mentor.

But even with all these elaborately laid plans, I kept thinking, "Who's going show up for this festival?" So, when I looked out of the third floor window of the AFI Silver Theatre offices on the first day and saw lines formed all the way down the street (snaking around the construction zones), I was floored. And then I thought, "Maybe we're on to something here…"

To top it off, like all good showmen (or women), I knew we needed a "big finish." We needed more than just a closing night film. We needed a moment to bring the community together to reinforce a much larger statement about the core mission of the festival, which was to truly create a "film-driven campfire" around which people from all sectors—the industry, the press, and the public—could circle to celebrate the non-fiction form. So we shut down Georgia Avenue, which is the state highway that ran between the AFI and Discovery headquarters and built a half-pipe for the great skateboarder Tony Hawk to do his amazing high-flying act. For several hundred children we screened a documentary about his "Boom Boom HuckJam show," again reinforcing the connection between "real life" and "real life on the screen" (in this case obviously geared towards the least anticipated of documentary audiences—kids). I had hoped that around 4,000 people would come out for Hawk's live show, but nearly three times that number crowded around his half pipe on a stunningly beautiful Sunday. Silver Spring hadn't seen that kind of celebration in decades.

That, to me, is what documentary can do for a community.

So that also enlightens me on your initial programming strategy—creating big events to get people there. How did that change over time?

The first year we had 1,000 submissions. The following year we had 2,000 submissions. By year three, people stopped asking why we were doing this, and by year four, no one had any more suspicion about the AFI and Discovery partnership and thankfully had stopped asking whether Discovery was programming the festival. All of that progress was a real relief. But mostly people stopped asking why they should come to Silver Spring for a documentary festival—and that was the biggest blessing of all. In some ways, we fairly quickly gained legitimacy.

It certainly helped that in the second year, under the new Director Patricia Finneran, as I moved into Executive Producing the festival, we inaugurated the filmmakers' conference which drove the industry to the festival. The first year, as I said, most of the industry had stayed away. The only way I was able to convince Indiewire to attend to cover the festival that inaugural year was that I had bought out the sponsorship of the documentary strand on their website for the entire year. They were a fledgling publication and I told them I would pay for the branding for all of documentary-related content for 2003—but they had to send somebody to cover the festival. I was fortunate to have had the financial resources to do that.

Which brings us to the million-dollar question: What was your budget the first year?

$1.6 million. $1.2 million came from Discovery. $100,000 came from the Corporation for Public Broadcasting—they were a founding sponsor, so that was the buy-in from the public broadcasting sector. We had about $300,000 in other cash donations and in-kind services. In that sense, we obviously had a very large budget relatively speaking to most start-up festivals.

For the longest time, we had the reputation of being the festival where you could go and eat very elegantly presented mini lamb chops. We had spectacularly produced parties—and Discovery expected that they would be executed flawlessly. That was the deal. If we were going to have an opening or closing night party at the Discovery Headquarters, it had to be perfect. Discovery wanted us to represent them well as a corporate entity, and they wanted it to be beautiful. We were very attentive to those details.

On the AFI side, they were fine with a slightly funkier vibe. But honestly the AFI brand is also a huge international brand. So there was an expectation that all events, social and otherwise, had to be very well produced, very well-orchestrated. Everyone involved wanted festival attendees to feel like they were guests in our "home," which is what the AFI Silver Theatre truly was. It didn't have the beer and peanuts feel—and still doesn't.

Was the festival set up as a non-profit or for profit?

It is a non-profit. It's a program of the American Film Institute.

Did the festival have a separate board or a separate advisory board?

It didn't; the AFI Board of Trustees had oversight over the festival and its staff. After the first ten years of the festival, an advisory board was created to put some prestigious documentary names on the letterhead.

In that first year, what was your greatest surprise?

As I said, I worried that literally nobody would show up. I kept thinking, "who is going to come to this thing?" We were showing documentaries in Silver Spring, which seemed like a real outlier idea. This was before the golden age of documentary in which we currently live. So the idea that somebody would put down $10 to buy a ticket to go to a movie theater in a construction zone just didn't make logical sense to me.

But ultimately there was a real hunger for this kind of content and for the creation of a certain kind of community zeitgeist. I think we tapped into it with press, with marketing, and with a transit campaign that literally put buses on the street, and throughout the Metro system, advertising the existence of this festival throughout the main corridors of Washington, DC. We were inescapable as an event from the outset.

And as I said, for the community day with Tony Hawk, we had hoped that 4,000 people would show up. He was such a draw for kids and families that when 12,000 showed up, I was bowled over. It was massive. And unexpected. And really gratifying.

Were there any disappointments that first year?

Well sure. The industry didn't embrace us at all. You know, everybody wants to be loved by the industry. You want to be known as a "player." Again, I think there was a lot of suspicion of Discovery initially—and that didn't go away for a while.

And we had some production hiccups as the technology in the AFI Silver Theatre was very advanced even for the film industry at that time. At the world premier of My Architect, we were still trying to marry the worlds of digital and 35mm film. After the festival trailer video played, the projectionist hadn't figured out how to switch from digital to film, and the trailer played over and over again in a loop over the film projection. I called up to the booth and ordered them stop the film. I announced to the audience that we were starting the film all over again—that it was a film that needed to be seen from its very first frame without interference. The audience just exploded in applause. They realized the technical difficulties that we were encountering and appreciated that we were not going to allow them to somehow impinge on their viewing experience. Still, one hates it when anything like that happens.

And there is the stuff you can't control, but make the best of. There were torrential downpours, as there frequently are in DC in June, and the theater was hit by lightning, knocking out our electricity—the entire theater went dark. During the NFL tailgate party, we all had to cram famous football players and the audience into a small tent, making for a "very intimate affair."

There were parts of that first festival that felt as if we were making it up as we went along. But you know I'm a documentary filmmaker, and that's what filmmaking is frequently all about. It felt like a film shoot!

How do you define success?

I define success by how emotionally connected people are to the experience. You have to continually challenge yourself, asking how can you create an experience around a film that is a moment in time that can never be captured again. From the instant that the lights go down to the moment when they come back up, every aspect of that experience has to be meaningful and central to the emotional state of everyone involved: from the audience, to the filmmaker, to the sponsor, and even to the people who are behind the scenes. What happens in that theater has to be so special that it can only be had in a festival. It has to feel as if somehow you've touched magic.

That is beautiful. I agree about the magic. Yes, anyone can watch a movie at home or on–the-go. Festivals are for creating an unforgettable experience. What are you most proud of?

I think the biggest challenge was—and is—how to create an authentic experience that is unique and true to the Washington, DC area.

Festivals always strive for that inner soul that becomes the expression of their own festival experience. True/False is sui generis to Columbia, Missouri. Full Frame is wholly "of" Durham, North Carolina. Somehow we had to identify what the soul of Silverdocs was going to be. I was not content with, "Oh, it's going to be a political film festival since we're in Washington, DC." That seemed to me a supreme cop-out. Washington, DC is full of neighborhoods and communities and organizations and special interests and people who love art and music and sports—and social issues, the environment and politics—everything that is represented in the filmic form.

If we were identified as the political film festival because we were in Washington, DC, that would have been a fail. It was for this reason that I chose a sports strand, not a political strand for that first year. I wanted to make a statement that this film festival is about the broad community of interests that is documentary film—and Washington, DC. And I think we succeeded in doing that.

So you are no longer with the festival. Why did you decide to move on?

After the first year, we hired Patricia Finneran to replace me as Festival Director. I went back to my regular job as being a filmmaker and film professor. I stayed on for six more years as the Executive Producer of the festival. After a couple of years, Sky Sitney was brought on board as head programmer —and she really took the festival into maturation. In the first years we saw the festival grow from a neonatal form, through childhood, into the gawky teenage years, and it is obviously now a very fully formed adult. Over time, there really wasn't a need any more for an executive producer role.

What are the challenges facing the future of film festivals?

Redundancy.

I said throughout my time at Silverdocs that out of 2,000 films we would get every year, 1,500 of them probably should never have been made—they had such profound problems with them that the filmmakers either shouldn't have made them, or they should have worked harder, or they should have had more experience in filmmaking before trying to be a director. That leaves 500 films or so that are really, really good. And of those 500 films, you figure Sundance, South by Southwest, Tribeca and the big boys are only going to screen a total of 150, maybe 200 of them at the most. That leaves at least 300 great, undiscovered films.

From a documentarian's point of view, it bothers me that festivals have lost a certain kind of imagination about what documentary can be—and about what kind of artistic risks that it should take. There are literally hundreds of undiscovered films and yet festivals are landlocked by predilections about who's making these films, and where have they played, and what kind of "social issue" function that they believe a documentary needs to serve. So programmers go with "the known" and not with "the potential." You shape and grow an audience's appreciation of the form by intensely engaging the latter. You pander to the industry, to people's egos, and to people's smug sense of self-righteousness by doing the former. To me, that is just profoundly disappointing.

I would agree that there are many amazing films that, unfortunately, never get seen on a big screen because they can't find the right festival. Or the right festival is more concerned with the name than the product.

I understand that you really want to have "big names" at your festival. But when I talk about the magic of the moment—when you bring a new vision or talent to the forefront for others to discover and believe in—that is what festivals should be known for. Many of the more well-known filmmakers make some wonderful films, but they're not necessarily exclusive to creating the type of magic that I'm advocating for.

Therefore, I think that a festival's lassitude and derivativeness doesn't serve filmmakers, and it certainly doesn't serve the audience. Festival directors and programmers need to take the time and care in finding those amazing gems, within those hundreds of films that don't have a marquis director or some industry presence behind them. It's really hard work but festival organizers need to be obsessed with discovering the new, the interesting, and the innovative voice speaking on a subject and in a context that has never before been witnessed. And then they need to shape an entire in-theater experience that will raise the characters and content found within the film to even greater heights. That's what makes magic and electrifies an audience.

That's fantastic—and inspiring. I think that many new festival directors are so concerned with the minutia, that the big picture, the desire to create a magic moment, is something they hope will happen, but do not necessarily plan in a way to ensure it.

Any last words of wisdom for someone who wants to start to a film festival?

People frequently want to start a film festival because they think it's a hip and cool—and they, themselves, want to be sitting at the table with the hip, cool, "in" crowd. Many film festivals have become very self-aware and self-conscious—which is a very inward-looking motivation. The question should be an external one: what are you going to do to deliver a festival experience that is unparalleled, not replicated, and not replicable? If you hold on to that goal as your driver, you'll inspire magic.

PAULA ELIAS
Citizen Jane Film Festival

Paula Elias is a consultant, public speaker and writer with extensive expertise on the gender inequities facing women in film. She has almost twenty years of experience in working with film festivals and creating women's initiatives. As Executive Director of the Citizen Jane Film Institute, which includes the Citizen Jane Film Festival, CJ Film Series and Camp Citizen Jane, a filmmaking camp that teaches young women the tools of filmmaking. In 2005, the festival was selected as one of the Top 25 Coolest Film Festivals in the World by *MovieMaker Magazine*. During her tenure, she grew the festival by more than 500 percent. She is the founder of the Citizen Jane Summit, a conference on gender parity now in its third year. Paula owns the boutique-advertising agency, Axiom, and also writes about film for the blog Seed&Spark.com.

Before you started at the Citizen Jane Film Festival, what were you doing?

I actually have a marketing background. I was Creative Director for a national media company and then started an advertising agency and worked on various marketing and creative campaigns. Five years before I came to Citizen Jane, I worked with True/False Film Festival, and really grew to love the idea of screening films I felt were important and got really excited about films made by women.

So you loved films. How did you turn that into a festival?

Citizen Jane Institute has an interesting genesis because we are affiliated with Stephens College, one of the oldest women's colleges in the country. One of the film professors was frustrated because she felt that for film students, "if you can't see it, you can't be it," meaning that if the students couldn't see any women in roles of power in film, they could not achieve that goal. We really wanted to bring women who were actively working in the industry to Missouri to mentor young filmmakers.

Citizen Jane began as a day-long lecture series where we could show snippets of films and talk about the careers of a few filmmakers. Then we got this crazy idea that we could do something a little bigger, where we could show some films, bring in some filmmakers, and maybe have a party. Over the past eight years, we added a Film Series and a Camp to teach young women the tools of filmmaking.

Our first year was very challenging, relatively chaotic. There were three of us working together, but you know that three heads are always challenging. It always seems like a great idea, the more the merrier, but it can be difficult. I have great respect for the two women that I worked with; both are incredibly creative and dedicated filmmakers. I think one of the biggest challenges for us was that we were so careful of each other, we didn't want to hurt anybody feelings, so nothing got done. At least, that is how I felt as a "take action, let's get it done" kind of person.

From the moment the three of you decided to put on a film festival to the actual event, how long was your planning process?

I actually came on a month before the festival. Kerri Yost, one of the other organizers, was just trying to go from a lecture series to something with a little bit more, while Polina Malikin, the third organizer, who's also a filmmaker and married to one of the co-founders of True/False, thought, "I have all these friends and I can bring all these people." She had big ideas. So Kerri was thinking small and Polina was thinking big, and there was no budget at all. It was a month out from the festival and they hadn't done any outreach or publicity at all. I had a strong relationship with Stephens College because I had run the Stephens Film Institute and had produced a film at Stephens, and I had this marketing firm, so they asked me to get the word out.

It was a really sweet little festival, and it was amazing that it was as successful as it was because people were doing this very part-time, coming from a total labor of love. I remember working on the printed program at two o' clock in the morning a few nights before opening. It was ridiculous. A lot of sweat equity.

I'm definitely an idealist: I was really impassioned by the idea that women are more than 51 percent of the population, yet are grossly underrepresented in film, one of the most powerful cultural mediums that we have. Film is the way that we convey culture to each other, and to the world. If women's stories aren't represented, that's a big problem. I believe that some of the problems we are facing as a country, and as a world, from environmentalism to poverty, need to be discussed by everyone at the same table. If you are only hearing from a very small representation of who we are, particularly middle-aged white men, you are only getting a piece of the puzzle. You are not hearing from people of color, you are not hearing from women, you are not hearing from people who grew up without money, and you are not hearing from gay, lesbian and transgender people—all who come from different experiences. I think it's crucial that we hear what they have to say. So, I was totally on board with the mission.

As we moved into the second year, I approached Kerri and said, "I love this. This is something that I really believe can change the world. It needs to happen." She agreed that the previous year was kind of a chaotic mess, and that having a co-director would be a good idea. A two-headed monster was easier to tame than a three-headed beast.

We had very different, but complimentary strengths. Kerri brought so much to the table, as an organizer and detail person; I was the big-idea, get-it-done person. Together, we could do anything. Even so, it was challenging. We did everything from logistics to programming, party planning to fundraising. All still part-time.

A few years ago, Stephens College finally asked us, "Who owns this thing? Who owns the festival? We are a part of it, but what is happening with it? So, we had a conversation and I said, "I just want it to happen and if you guys will fund it then that's great." They graciously agreed, and we were able to really grow quickly and significantly. I came on full time with Stephens, and Kerri stepped back to do just programming. We still got the chance to work together and build it, but with separate and finite responsibilities. While we've grown 500 percent since our inception, I don't think it will ever be a huge festival because of the niche that we have. It's been a pretty wild ride.

For your first event, did you know who your audience was?

No. I don't even think anybody had a conversation about audience. I literally came in a month before, and thought, "Just get some people here. We made the thing and we are not even sure what it is. Just bring some people!" It was useful that I have a strong marketing background, so I was able to bring that to the table and figure out a quick, first-year plan.

Who is the core patron now? Has knowing this information changed your programming strategy?

It's something that I think that we refine every year. Certainly in the beginning, we had the idea that because we were a big college town with the main campuses of Missouri University, Stephens College, and Columbia College, we thought we would have a strong collegiate following. As it turns out, college students make up about 30 percent of our audience, which for many events is really high. Our primary audience is women over 40, followed by our collegiate audience. Surprisingly, or maybe not surprisingly, about a third of our audience is men. After all these years, I think we have a definite idea about who our audience is.

After the first year, I had done research to get an idea about the types of programs that people really embraced. I was surprised that films not necessarily of the highest technical quality, but with great, compelling stories, often brought in the most phenomenal audiences. It's a balance. We want to make sure that we have high quality films because we definitely want to fight the perception that women can't make great films so we need to make sure we show really great movies, but our primary focus is on featuring great stories that are told well. Seeking out these films has certainly shaped our programming.

That first year, how many days was the festival, and how many films did you screen?

In 2008, we had 39 films. Eight of them were features, 31 were shorts. They were shown over three days.

And last year? How many venues? The audience?

In 2014, we screened 74 films: 15 features and 59 shorts. About 6,500 people attended throughout the weekend at five venues. It really has blossomed.

Do you remember what the budget was for the first year?

It was almost non-existent. It really wasn't a budget. We just applied for a couple of grants and crossed our fingers.

What has it grown to?

Last year our budget was around $100,000 which covers the operating costs and slight increases for our team leaders.

Are you are paid as an employee in the university?

Yes. Salary support is not part of the budget.

Is the festival a registered non-profit?

Since the festival is now part of the college, technically it is. That was one of the questions we discussed a few years ago: whether this would be a separate entity, or part of the school.

For the first few years, how did you run the organization?

It was a little bit of an unclear relationship. Basically we went off and did whatever we needed to do, and got whatever funding we could. Certainly, the college was very supportive with venues. That's been a great thing. We don't have to pay rent, which is a major expense for most festivals.

Because you are not a non-profit, you don't have a governing board. Do you have an advisory board?

Now, that is an interesting point because we are going through a shift where the college wants to get a better handle on what has been happening and how the event has been organized. Over the years, they trusted me to manage it, and it's been successful and grown.

They have brought in a team of people to help bridge a better relationship between the event and the college. They have been very supportive.

Has that been helpful?

You know, festival work is really solitary. It's kind of a weird hybrid when I think about what makes the perfect director: somebody who loves people, but can sit twelve hours in front of the computer and not be bothered by that. You have to be "on" and be able to present in front of people, but also not care if everybody else takes the credit. So it's nice to have some more people thinking about the festival with me.

That's an interesting perspective. I ask about boards because some events have as few as three members, and others as many as two dozen. Some members are active, others are passive. But to me, it's all about being supportive. It sounds like you are finally getting that support.

Back to that first year, other than the worry that no one would show up, what were your biggest fears?

I was afraid it was going to be a train wreck because it was not the most well organized experience. We didn't really have any funding. We didn't really have any overall plan. We just said, "Hey, let's do this."

It's a hard rollercoaster ride, but that's sometimes how great things happen. I mean if you knew how bad it could be, I don't know if you would do it.

The community really supported us. We have great people in the community who came forward and really gave their blessings and support to make this happen too.

What was the greatest surprise?

My greatest surprise? How much work it really is. I have a lot of experience managing events. I worked for True/False for five years from the time when they were small to when they exploded, so I really felt quite confident. I felt really comfortable with my ability to put on the festival. Still, I was shocked by how much work it is. There is no finance person under me, there is no operation manager under me, so basically, I have a hand in every single thing that happens.

If somebody drops out, it's me who picks up the slack. I do everything from helping to program the films, to making sure that filmmakers arrive on time. I mean, I don't usually pick someone up at the airport, but I am certainly willing if that has to happen. It's about picking up trash, sweeping the floor, talking a volunteer down who's having a meltdown, greeting the filmmakers, introducing the films, talking to the sponsors, even making sure there is wine at the VIP reception. It all falls to me. It can be exhausting.

We have a midnight breakfast on Saturday night after our big dance party, and it's a blast. People from 18 to 65, fresh off the dance floor, meeting at a local restaurant for a late night bite. Last year, when I arrived, I saw that the room was full of filmmakers, filmgoers and sponsors, but no food! The cook had made two casseroles. He was in the back smoking, so I went out and asked, "What is going on?" He responded, "Oh, two people didn't come in, so that's all I had time to make." I replied, "I'm sorry but that's not possible, it's not workable."

We did what we had to do. I strapped on an apron, threw two more to my son and his girlfriend, and we started to wash dishes and flip eggs and sausage and tofu. It was just ridiculous. We were throwing out plates as quickly as we could. For me, that is the commitment you have to make.

When things are beyond your control, you still have to make it happen. You live and breathe the festival. There are not enough hours in the day. There is always more work to do, and just when you think you're done, another crisis arises, and you go back into fix-it mode.

How do you separate your personal and professional life? Do you find balance?

For me, it really has been about drafting everybody I love to work along side me, because I have been working 24/7. Get your significant other to love it as much as you do, and volunteer to help. Draft your kids if you've got them, and draft all your friends, so while you are working, you get to be around the people you love.

Do you see yourself at Citizen Jane forever?

I have been thinking this year if this is that "something" I want to do for the rest of my life. You know this is crazy work. I do love it. It's fun, and it's so gratifying. It's the most satisfying thing I've ever done—but I'm not sure that I want to work at this pace forever. I love the fact that we are a part of shining the light on women and the films they make, providing support to these filmmakers and helping to get their films made. I will definitely continue to work to help women's voices be heard. I can see myself working to develop women's initiatives with other festivals and other organizations. I have had several conversations about consulting with other festivals.

Three years ago, I created the Citizen Jane Summit, a conference focused on bringing thought leaders together from around the country to focus on the obstacles standing in the way of women being heard in film and media. I really felt the need to do something more than just screen films and Citizen Jane seemed like the perfect opportunity to move beyond just celebrating women filmmakers to focusing on how to really affect change. The CJ Summit has been really inspiring. The statistics around the representation of women in film haven't moved above the single digits in more than ten years and I am confident that the only way we will see real change is by building a community of people focused on the solution.

The thing that I've learned at Citizen Jane is that I want to be doing something with my time here on earth that feels powerful and meaningful. So the next thing for me is to do something that I really believe in, perhaps something that I don't have to build from scratch. I am excited about getting the chance to use the things I have learned to help more organizations on a more global scale. I feel like I got Citizen Jane to a good, mature space, and I'm proud of it, and proud of all the work everybody has done.

What are your biggest ongoing challenges with the festival?

I think for Citizen Jane, the biggest challenge is the vision, and who gets to decide what that vision is. You know, we are at a level of maturity and some of those questions really need to be answered, while integrating a rogue, community-built and grassroots film festival into a 200-year old organization. While we all want the same thing, the methods and the plan for getting to our goals vary greatly.

This is an issue for many small events that are tied up with larger institutions. We both know at least a few others.

Right. Your hands are tied in just the most bizarre way. It is a long process, but in the end, the results can be worth the agony.

What is one of the sticking points?

I think, the biggest challenge is figuring out who gets to decide what the vision is. Festival work is really just community building and I believe that building our community based on a model of collaboration, where all the stakeholders have a voice is integral to our success. When people feel ownership and that their voices count, they will ensure a successful event.

While Citizen Jane has grown by double digits every year, it is a growth that has been gradual and evolutionary. We are in the same town as True/False, an event that has audiences of more than 35,000 people. We don't want that. That would be counter to what we are trying to achieve: a community event that connects filmmakers and audiences in intimate settings.

Every year, someone suggests that we have a private VIP lounge for the filmmakers. I respond that we just spent $600 to bring a filmmaker to town, and I want them to be able to connect with filmmakers and filmgoers. It's why the festival was created. We are building a community, so why would I put them in a little room?

We take filmmakers on nature hikes, we give them massages; it's a very chill experience. If we had 20,000 people, that would ruin it.

In what way has the festival exceeded your original vision?

I am kind of stunned that we've been able to pull off something so lovely. I love Citizen Jane, and when I look at it, I think it's a fantastic thing. I know that filmmakers really feel supported here; they feel connected to other filmmakers and to their audiences in ways that doesn't often happen. And our town embraces the whole thing. I mean when you live in the middle of the country there aren't as many opportunities for this type of interaction. There is this lovely innocence to that and appreciation.

I'm really pleased that we almost sold out our 1,200 seats on opening night theater two years in a row. I feel proud of that.

And of course, we've shown films that have gone on to do some pretty incredible things. When we showed *Tiny Furniture*, half our audience hated it, and the other half totally got it. A couple of years later, Lena Dunham became a big name, and they all remembered the film very fondly.

I am also proud that we've been risky in our programming. We've shown films that people would not get a chance to see any other way. We've shown Native American films that show almost nowhere. We've shown *An Ordinary Life*, a narrative film about date rape, that was a U.S. Premier. I don't know that I've ever seen a fiction film about date rape. It was done so elegantly and so beautifully by director Audrey Estrougo. It was a difficult subject matter that had not really screened anywhere else.

When Audrey arrived, she was kind of prickly: "Okay I'm here in this festival in Missouri. I don't know anyone. I don't even know what I'm doing. I've been working so hard. Nobody supports me and this is hard to do." It is hard. Making a film is hard. Being a woman and making film is really hard. Making the film about that subject matter? It had to be really hard.

I made it my personal challenge to just love her up. I just wanted to soften her up and make her really love being here. We became good friends over the weekend. It just felt great to be able to give back.

Audrey told a story that was really crucial. We need to hear that story. I feel that through the auspices of Citizen Jane, we were able to give something back to her. That is one of the most important things that we offer, to refuel the filmmakers so they can go out and do more amazing things.

How do you define success?

As a festival?

In relation to anything. What's success to you?

You're getting all deep on me. I would have answered this differently a year ago. I think, for me personally, success is peace. By that I mean, I've always been one of those people who does a lot; it's interesting to me to have all these things going on. If I have any downtime at all, I start another project. I like to get a lot done. I get a lot of satisfaction out of that.

I think I'm finally learning how to streamline my life so that while I'm getting a lot done, I'm also getting a lot of satisfaction. I'm contributing a lot but not having the panic that goes along with it. I probably spent the first six years with the festival with my stomach in knots trying to figure out how we were going to pay for the festival, coordinate venues, locate missing films. You know, the last minute stuff that pops up and takes over the day. I think it's a real challenge to figure out how to handle that on a personal level. I am grateful my husband and kids are supportive. Even though I don't spend as much time and attention on them as I probably should, they're understanding.

So success for me is just figuring out how to live my life in a way that I feel good about, while maintaining integrity. That makes me feel at peace.

What are you most proud of? What DNA have you implanted into the festival that you think will carry forward the longest, or that you think has the biggest impact?

I'm most proud of the community I helped create. To me, that is a really important job. I think it's what festival work is ultimately about: community building. It's about creating experiences, whether they are screenings, panels, discussions, parties, or workshops —where people can come together and connect in lasting ways. I've never seen anything create that like a festival.

I feel that's at the core of my job. I want to help create a place in the world where women's voices are celebrated and supported. I think Citizen Jane does that. I'm really proud of that.

What challenges do you see for the future of film festivals in general?

Well, sometimes I think there are a heck of a lot of film festivals, and it is critical to define who you are and what you stand for. It goes back to marketing, really. If you are really clear about who you are, where you plan to go, what you are trying to do, and who is going with you, there will be a place for you.

I think the challenge is always refining why are we here. If we don't have a reason for being here, let's not trump one up. Let's not create one. I think festivals, or any endeavor, can get into trouble trying to sustain themselves just to sustain themselves.

If you have a purpose and you are still serving it, and the people that you're trying to serve still need it, then just get better at it. Just do that better. If you're not serving a purpose anymore, then quit and do something else. If women make one out of every two films, would we still need a Citizen Jane? Just be really clear about your purpose, what you are supposed to be doing, and making sure that you do that as well as you can every day.

What words of wisdom do you have for someone who wants to create a film festival?

Run.

That's the number one answer by the way.

I bet it is. I don't know if I would have words of wisdom but I would just ask them "why?" Get really clear about why you want to do it. If you think it just seems fun, there is no question that there are times it is absolutely the best ride I have ever been on. However, there have also been some of the most horrible times as well. I mean, incredible stress. You must have nerves of steel to be able to run a film festival. You do. All the while, not showing anybody how stressful it is. My main piece of advice is to be really clear about why you want to do it.

It seems like some people think, "Ooh, film festivals! That's the new thing. Let's do one of those." I don't think that's how it should be. I think there should be some really solid center that compels you to do it, because that's what will sustain you when the times get tough. It will get tough.

Your "why" must be big enough to let you stay up 24 hours at a time, to let you lose all of your friends because you have no time to be with them, or because you ask them one too many times to do something for you for the festival. Your "why" must be big enough to get you to ask people over and over again for money, and face constant rejection. To sustain you when you have 1,200 people waiting and watching a film and you can't get the damn Blu-ray disc to play. If your why is that big, then yes, you should start a film festival.

Measure all of the worst-case scenarios against your "why," and if that "why" is big enough, then start your festival. I feel like that's true.

DANIEL SOL
Holly Shorts Film Festival

With a passion for film and filmmaking since childhood, Daniel Sol decided to move to California in 2000. After working on commercial productions as a production assistant and then acting in various films, he gained a deep understanding of the filmmaking process. Sol realized that young filmmakers had very little access to industry professionals, and few options for screening their films. And thus, the Holly Shorts Film Festival was born. Daniel also battled daily with domestic exhibitors as a theatrical sales manager at Lionsgate for six years (2008-2013), and in 2008 he produced and starred in the indie feature film Night Before the Wedding.

What was your background before you started the Holly Shorts Film Festival?

The idea started in 2004, but 2005 was our first festival, the first full year was for promoting and working on it. At the time I was at Cal State Northridge, actually studying Kinesiology, a whole different area of expertise. I started off in film school, but decided I didn't really enjoy the film school experience. That was partly what spawned the idea of doing the festival.

Film school just wasn't going well for me at Northridge. I was already working as a production assistant for an established filmmaker, learning everything on set that I was getting in school. I was making great contacts, and learning business from these guys that were doing it for twenty to forty years. I was a production assistant on TV shows and stuff, just assisting, even doing some stand-in jobs and extra jobs—the usual stuff in college, just doing whatever you can to get paychecks. I felt there was a need for people to form connections with the industry people that I was meeting. I knew working on some short films that this is something that was needed here in Los Angeles.

My brother was also an actor, and had a small theater called The Space. He directed and produced plays, and we'd always support the plays, help them build the sets, tape the shows. So we had a location, a forty-seat theater, and knew all we needed was a projector and a screen. We didn't have any money or anything to start—we just knew that we had this location, we had people who were eager, a lot of filmmakers from our jobs on set, and other people we knew. I felt this was something that we should start and try to do.

When you went into your first year, did you have a mission or an audience in mind?

A formal mission statement, no. A guiding principal, yes. People needed exposure. They needed that spot to be able to shine. We felt at the time that the Los Angeles Film Festival was not really a good home for short films. Los Angeles-based filmmakers were turning to events in Aspen, Palm Springs, and of course, Sundance. We felt that there was just not a great home for short films in Los Angeles.

We felt that we want to create a great spotlight for the short film maker, and then build an audience from there. So, that was the start: a forty-seat theater, two and a half days, 23 movies.

From there, we have grown exponentially. We moved to Cinespace, then to the Sunset 5, and finally to the famous Chinese Theater.

When you were planning that first year, did you have an audience in mind? Did you know who you were marketing the event to?

Our main focus was essentially young Hollywood. We're in Los Angeles, so we could also have people attending from other places, but for the start, it was targeted to the young up-and-coming Hollywood people who are eager, who are learning and working in the business. In LA, if you're an actor you may also be a filmmaker, you may work with a filmmaker who works with this producer who knows this actor, this photographer or editor.

During that first event, what were some of your greatest fears?

Well, the biggest thing was that the projector kept working. The night before opening night, I was testing it at my house, and the bulb kept going out. After trying to fix it in vain, at 2:00 AM, we started to call companies that worked 24 hours to get us a new projector. As it turns out, it was just a power surge issue with the power cord we were using. Obviously now, we have theaters with professionals who handle these things.

My other fear was, "are people going to enjoy this?" Looking back, the quality of some films was, to be quite honest, pretty bad. Yes, we showed a few "known" films that had played Tribeca or Sundance. But some of the films were more in the low-budget side. This was before YouTube, before digital was where it is now, so production quality was little more than VHS quality. I was also nervous if people were going to hate this kind of thing, saying this is awful, that we're showing a film that we didn't personally love as much, but I had to program them—we didn't have much to choose from.

What was your greatest surprise during the festival?

The response to the films. From our standpoint, we were programming, thinking of quality, but not really sure about how they would play. Then the audience started really laughing—all the jokes were hitting, and people really enjoyed themselves. That was the start of the overall energy that carried the festival through. We realized that this was going to work. Every show sold out. That's why we kept going.

So your initial programming strategy was basically, "We have thirty submissions and need to screen twenty—so we're good." How has that changed over the years—how do you program today?

Early on we just wanted to show the best films we received. The first three or four years, we had a larger space, which allowed us to start selecting films differently. Obviously we're still trying to show the best films, but now we actually could program based on genre or theme. We were getting 300 to 400 submissions, and ended up showing approximately fifty movies in two days.

Now we are at the Chinese Theater for a full ten days, and can program based more on theme and timing, especially since we are screening films day and night. We receive over 2,000 entries from around the world.

That happened pretty fast, but we still are programming only what we felt were the best of them, and there were only so many films. That garnered us reputation of, "Hey, we're showing some really good films, only the best will get in," so it's competitive. There's still a balance, but obviously as years go on, the philosophy can change. We've learned more how to program, what feels best to program, when you show films. It's something that we still learn as we go.

Is Holly Shorts set up as a non-profit organization?

No, we're not.

What was your decision to organize as a for-profit?

Kind of early on, we felt that we were going to get into other areas of business—potentially productions or distribution. For us, we have built this thing from the ground up and we wanted to keep it that way. We felt that with the rules and tax reporting of a nonprofit, and the necessity for a board of directors, it really was not the right route for us.

We have a soft board—people who help advise us, people who we talk with—but it's nothing that's official, or an entity that we must report to.

We've talked about creating a separate non-profit entity to work with youth filmmakers. It's something that we want to develop and do, but it's not something that we are actively pursuing. As the festival has grown and more work is piled onto our plate, it hasn't happened.

Because you are a for-profit entity, how do you raise money?

It's similar to a non-profit, except you can't easily access some donations or funds from sponsors and. Submissions, advertising, sponsorships, and ticket sales are essentially our main revenue sources. Of course there is some merchandise stuff too, but we haven't really gotten into the merchandise like Sundance or SXSW.

Since you're a for-profit, you don't have to disclose, but may I ask about your annual budget?

I haven't really looked at the full numbers for this year, it's probably in the $100K range.

Some would consider that a small festival, yet you show so many films and have such a large reputation.

Yes. The thing is, it looks like a much bigger event in scope and scale, but the budget is relatively low. We work with what we have—and use our resources wisely to make the most of what we have.

We barter for much of what we need: food, beverages, prizes and hotel rooms. If you added up the values from these partnerships, you could probably add another $500K to the budget.

We've always had to scrape and claw to make ends meet. When we were at the Egyptian Theater, we sacrificed ticket sales in exchange for rent. We had some huge events there, filling close to 700 seats because celebrities like Josh Brolin, Jessica Biel or Adrian Grenier were in attendance. People love a big red carpet event. Anyway, the decision was made to move to this large theater because we would get national coverage in the trades, and in the public media, such as E! and *Entertainment Tonight*. In the long run, that type of coverage has allowed us to grow—it was the splash that we needed to carry us forward for many years.

Because you're in Los Angeles, do you find it easier to attract celebrities to the event? Or do they show up because they just want to attend, like anyone else?

It is a mixture. Some come out because they may know a filmmaker who's screening, or they supported the film in some way. We recently had a screening where a stunt man who has been in the business for a very long time premiered his first short film. We didn't realize that he as so well connected, and were surprised when a slew of big-name actors and directors came to the screening. It was a shock—the good kind. People in the business want to support the films of their friends. They'll come out to the screenings, they come out all the time just to support and check out the films and network and mingle.

We also reach out to invite celebrities by contacting agents and managers. It's important to go through the proper channels: invitations, background information, what is the connection to the festival. But people in this town love red carpets. When you have a red carpet, all of a sudden you're getting requests from publicists and talent agents, "Hey my client is on this show, how do we do this? He wants to be on the carpet."

Being close to the action is helpful. There are many festivals outside of Los Angeles that must pay exorbitant appearance fees to bring in name talent.

I can't imagine paying someone to attend. I guess, I would have to weigh what the benefits are versus the amount of money we'd have to pay out. Would the benefit of additional press or increased attendance be worth it?

We do pay for incidentals, sometimes with varying results. One year, we honored Joe Carnahan, and hired a car for him for the night. I guess that after the event, he went out and partied all night long. The next day, we received a bill and were a bit surprised when we realized he'd taken the car all over town, getting wasted. It was pretty funny. But that stuff happens.

I wish we had the budget to fly talent in. People on the east coast often ask for us to fly them in. It is rare, but we've done it a few times here and there. For almost any filmmaker who comes from outside of Los Angeles, we try to help with hotels.

At what point did running the festival become a full-time job for you?

In 2013, I made the decision to leave my old job and concentrate on Holly Shorts. I was at Lionsgate for six years in sales and distribution. It was difficult balancing a full-time sales job with running the festival. It was pretty stressful and I had to make a choice. I thought, "OK, I'm either going to invest myself and go full-time with this, or I have to stay and commit my job." Obviously, I wanted to keep the festival going—that was always the goal. By this time, the festival had grown and we had larger attendance and awareness. That, combined with a little more money in the budget allowed me to make the decision.

What other full-time staff or part-time paid staff does the festival employ?

Not too many. Of course we have of course Theo Dumont, who is the co-founder and works as our publicist. He has a PR firm, so he takes care of public relations, the red carpet and media outreach. And we have Nicole Castro, who is our part-time Managing Director. She is paid seasonally, but she's around helping out year-round, even though she is based in New York. She manages the volunteers, keeps us organized, serves as the liaison with the filmmakers and does an incredible job with them.

Then we have other folk that are part-time or we pay them on an event-by-event basis, like our digital guy who manages all the files, trailers, our YouTube channel, our DailyMotion channel—anything related to digital. He is in Austin. Our Social Media Director is based in Portland. And we have another social media person who blasts messages from his base in London. Plus three or four people who work on sponsorships and partners. They are all over. It's a very international team.

What about your review team?

Surprisingly, the selection committee is a very small team—eight to twelve of us, plus a few interns who have a passion for content and programming. We assign films to everyone and they watch and recommend. While we watch a majority of the films, there are certain programs where we bring in special judges—such as for documentaries. We have really great doc screeners who are the industry's doc pros.

Out of 1,200+ submissions, how many are you, personally, watching?

The majority of them. I take on most of the programming and most of the film screening, even though we all divide assignments up, and watch a great number together. We get together once every week or every other week and we'll watch as many films as we can—upwards of sometimes 70 to 100 in a day. We track everything in a Google document where reviewers put their scores and notes.

That is very ambitious. I feel lazy watching only the top-rated 350 films.

Actually, DC Shorts has a great process that allows filmmakers to access their reviews and scores. I wish we had something like that.

With only eight to twelve reviewers, how do you keep them interested?

That has been an issue in the past, especially when we had more reviewers. We would get requests from people from film enthusiasts to big-time agents. But when the work needed to be done, they disappeared, or had too many issues navigating the back ends of Withoutabox or Film Freeway. Ultimately, we found that we could get more work done with a small, dedicated committee, than with a larger set of well-meaning but ineffective volunteers.

What do you do to develop your audience?

It's an ever-fluid scenario for us. We get large audiences for most shows, but our repeat business is very small. Most of the films are supported by friends and family, so they bring in audiences who are there primarily to see only a single film. Right now, the big questions are, "how do we bring people back, and what incentives do we use?" For our monthly screenings, we give away cool prizes and drink specials. That helps to cultivate an audience to keep coming back month after month.

For the main event, it is more difficult. Obviously, they're on the newsletter list and they get our emails and may come back at some point, maybe twice a year. We need an audience retention plan for so many reasons—planning, fundraising, and refining our mission.

Which leads me to ask, what are some of your biggest challenges today?

It goes back to sponsorship. Again we're not a non-profit, so we have certain sponsors that don't want to, or can't do stuff with a for-profit entity. Since incoming funds cannot come from the corporate foundations, it must come from their marketing budgets. If you are not already a budget item, getting that designation is very difficult. That said, we do well enough, and we have some great long-term sponsors who know that being in front of our audience means increased business for them. As I mentioned earlier, we receive a large amount of product that we use for prizes and parties. But to keep the lights on, cash is the only currency the electric company accepts.

Programming is another challenge, especially now because the quality of submissions we receive are better than ever. Making those decisions is difficult, and often gut wrenching.

Talk about some programs you've implemented that have been successful?

Our monthly screening series has surpassed my expectations. We are able to screen even more films—sometimes films that we were unable to find a slot for in the main festival. Filmmakers love the extra chances to screen their materials, and audiences really like to discover new content.

Have you had to kill a program because it just did not perform to your satisfaction?

One thing that comes to mind right off the bat are our student programs. We have no intention of stopping them—they are important in our long-term vision—but getting high-quality student-created content, especially at the high school level, has been very difficult. Maybe we are not sexy enough for students to want to send us entries. The other part of the equation is that audiences are not super psyched to watch a whole program of student works. Their expectations are lower, and many would prefer to watch such content online, if at all. Last year, we programmed the student shows on Saturday, our busiest day, and we promoted the screening with greater intensity than any other program, but in the end, that audience did not show up. I'm not throwing in the towel, but I know we need to rethink the program before it becomes a burden.

We don't screen student films separately. I would worry that audiences are predisposed to think of student work as inferior. Which we both know is too bad, since many are incredible—even better than those made by well-known filmmakers.

That's a good point. And it's true —so many of these student films are actually better than some of the big-budget shorts we see from around the world. People see the word "student," and they don't want to be bothered. We want Hollywood to embrace these films. There's just a certain element that they're looking for as far as the industry goes, certain standards.

Films that we love sometimes elicit only lukewarm reactions with an audience, their reaction is lukewarm. It is disappointing when you have such high expectations, and those are not matched. I can understand films that we know from the get-go are not to our audiences' taste, but when we think we found a home run, and it barely gets a single, I have to wonder.

That happens to us a bit, too. Years ago, I realized that I liked films for very different reasons that the audience. That is one of the reasons I must trust the review system and reviewers' recommendations. Unlike Holly Shorts, DC Shorts has 80-100 reviewers, most of who are dedicated audience members or local filmmakers. I have to believe that if they like a film, the audience as a whole will also.

Where do you see the festival in five years?

We are focusing and working on the digital side of things, such as having an online film festival, and creating or branding an existing digital platform for short content. Everything is going the way of apps and online—people watch a great deal of content on small screens such as tables and even smartphones. With the online landscape exploding, we feel we have to participate in that to some degree. It has helped us grow in the past. Why else are there more submissions and films being made? Because new filmmakers now have the access to the equipment and software—online or through using their personal devices.

I'd like to see us expand our programming. I know we can never show 700 films—there's only so big you can get. But we can make the experience better and bigger, adding more screens, which should attract more people. I am often asked if we will ever get into feature films. Probably not, although we currently screen a feature as part of our closing program—usually a film from a festival alumnus. We could move more into TV and webisodes—both content that is short.

And finally, I'd like to see us travel with the Festival. We want to take it to other cities, potentially places like New York, London and Miami. We are already working on a plan for Miami, so that will be a good test. We did drive-in pop-ups in Austin and New York last year, so that's another area of growth as well.

How do you define success? It does not have to be about Holly Shorts, but how do you define success for you?

Whatever it is, a film festival or making a film, starting a business, having a kid, whatever you're doing in life, it's about doing it to the fullest you can —having your passion behind it. With that will come success. You have to believe in what you're doing, and do it fully.

Success is also making an impact. In the past, we've been able to connect filmmakers with producers and agents. When those connections work out, and someone starts to succeed on their own, I get very excited. Those type of success stories are a little corny, but it's the truth. If we didn't care about them, then there's no point running a festival where we're showcasing films.

What are you most proud of? What DNA have you injected into the formation of the festival that you think will have the biggest impact in the future?

There are a few things. I think just being able to say that we were able to establish the festival and keep growing—and to still be here eleven years later. For us it's a big deal. You don't often have the time to reflect, and sadly, there are so many years it was just a blur. Sometimes, you have to stop and reflect a little bit and appreciate things. A lot of times in life we don't do that.

Personally, I am most proud of the panels and discussions that allow all filmmakers the chance to make lasting industry connections. It's almost like its own little festival. Since we're in Los Angeles, we have access to a lot of great industry people. We're lucky to have that pool to invite them out to speak. If you have folks coming internationally or from out of town, they definitely want access to industry professionals while they're here. The whole idea started very organically, and it has turned out to be our number one asset.

What challenges do you see for the future of film festivals?

It depends on what happens with cinema. I know there is a lot of discussion about the industry moving online and speculation that cinemas are going to die. I feel there's always going to be a need and place for blockbusters and Hollywood to have a home for their films. I feel like people still want the festival experience. And being in a big, lush theater enhances that experience. Yes, you can see some of the films online or on video, but it's nothing like seeing it with the audience, with the response, meeting the filmmaker face to face, and seeing the filmmaker discuss their craft. That whole thing still feels relevant.

For us in short films, I think we're in a good place. More short films are being made than ever before. Filmmakers need a place to showcase their talent that has legitimacy, and in front of decision makers. Only festivals can provide that.

Final question: what are your words of wisdom for someone who wants to start a film festival?

I would say that if you don't love films, and especially if you don't love filmmakers, then do not start a film festival. It seems very obvious, but I think you'd be surprised that so many festivals seem to not like filmmakers. They have a disdain or lack of respect, or a weird bitter relationship happening. On top of that, it's a business based on passion.

If you have the wrong mindset going in: if you think, "Oh I'm just going to do this. It's going to be a huge thing," or if you are doing it for material gain, and it will fail. We have all seen many festivals that have come and gone. People don't realize the amount of work and time that goes into trying to build an audience, trying to get the word out, making sure things run smoothly. So many things can go wrong—how do you handle that? If your mindset isn't right, you just shouldn't do it. Don't do it.

SARA BERESFORD
EcoFocus Film Festival

Sara Beresford is the Festival Director and Programmer for EcoFocus Film Festival. Sara grew up in the Seattle area and moved to Athens, GA in 1997 to earn a master's degree in Conservation Ecology and Sustainable Development. She subsequently moved to Washington, DC to work for an international environmental non-profit organization. While traveling to remote corners of the globe, she had some time to gaze at her navel, and, among other things, decided that she didn't have to be directly involved in science to make an impact. EcoFocus Film Festival was born out of that idea. Sara believes that film is an effective way to engage people about important issues, and loves the way film can bring together a community around a festival.

What was your background before you started the EcoFocus Film Festival?

Before I started the festival, I didn't have a background in film other than a keen interest—no experience, training, education, nothing. I was working almost entirely in the environmental non-profit world. The festival originated from my thinking about utilizing environmental films, especially documentaries, to effectively inform and inspire people.

Tell us about the creation story for EcoFocus.

The Dean of the School of Ecology at the University of Georgia, where I got my master's degree, tracked me down when he found out I had recently moved back to town. A mutual friend and I had gone to dinner and I'd said that while I was thinking about my next professional steps, I had this "aha" moment in realizing that visual media and the arts were an exciting thing to think about in terms of outreach to the public. I guess he was working for the Dean at the time and they must have had a conversation. So the dean reached out to me, knowing I had a background in non-profit work and management and said, "You know, we are thinking about forming this environmental film festival and haven't thought about it much beyond that." He asked me if I would make it happen. I literally went home from that meeting and Googled "environmental film festival."

That's how it started. I had to figure it out as I went along, and it took about three years alone to set the format that I felt was most effective for our particular audience. For those three years or so I felt I was "cooking along," but there were a lot hard lessons learned in the meantime.

How long was that first planning period from "aha" moment to first screening?

That first planning period was approximately ten months, which was pretty crazy. It happens that at the same time the Dean contacted me, a brand new arthouse cinema had just opened in Athens. The Athens community had struggled with supporting arthouse cinema; most ventures had failed to attract more than a teeny film audience. But a couple of years before I started the festival, a woman had taken an old tire recap plant and rebuilt it out into this beautiful cinema space. That happening at the same time this new Dean was looking for a way to reach out to the public that would reflect well on the school made both of those factors a part of the event's genesis.

You say that there's a small movie-going audience in Athens. Did you have an audience in mind when you were creating the first event?

I think the tricky thing about the EcoFocus audience is to reach and engage both the people who already are interested in the environment and environmental issues as well as the people for whom the information in the films and the stories is new. In other words: how do I make this niche environmental film festival reach beyond "preaching to the choir"?

I learned that the value of the festival was not just trying to get beyond that choir, but also creating a sense of community amongst that choir. And that became an incredibly important factor in how I defined the festival. Because if a bunch of individuals sitting in their houses looking at computer screens think of themselves as environmentalists, I suppose that has some value in terms of individual choices. But when all those people are sitting in a dark room together with 130 others and they're being inspired by same information, or pissed off by the same information, or whatever they're feeling, there is an intangible value to that—a creation of a sense of community amongst those people that is an important part of what I was trying to achieve.

I think when I first started I didn't really have a target audience in mind because I wanted to reach anyone who wanted to watch films and learn more about environmental issues. I had some naysayers at the beginning who doubted whether the festival could succeed. I remember that a couple people told me that this was just going to be sharing a bunch of environmental films to people who are already a self-selected group. I sort of felt that I had something to prove to the naysayers by showing them I could actually reach beyond the environmentalists.

My biggest surprise in terms of audience came from living in a town with 35,000 undergraduate students and a dominant university presence. I thought I would have a ready-made audience, but the students have been my toughest group of people to engage—to the point where even though student tickets are free, I still don't have fantastic student involvement. I have tried all these different ways to engage students. I've worked with faculty to have them offer extra credit to their students, I've offered free meals at the festival for students, I've shown films on the campus. But I've been surprised year after year by the difficulty in attracting large numbers of students. They come, but not in the numbers I expected. Students see themselves as busy, poor, and stressed-out, and coming to film festivals is not their highest priority, at least not in Athens.

In that first year, how many films did you screen? Over how many days?

The first year was a ten-day festival with 15 feature-length films and 25 shorts. The big difference in format that first year versus subsequent festivals is that I offered three or four opportunities to see each feature film. That was a mistake. They need to be given only one, maybe two opportunities. They need to be given a sense of urgency or exclusivity about a screening engagement. If they think they have three or four chances to see the film, they don't come; if there's only one chance, they make it a priority. I also stopped programming shorts in blocks after that first year. Instead I program the shorts with the features to make sure to get more eyes on those great short films. My audiences really like it that way, too. After a couple of different formats in the intervening years (believe it or not I did a 28-day festival), I ultimately landed on that ten-day format: two big weekends with weekday screenings and school visits scattered in between.

What was your greatest fear in the first year?

My greatest fear was that nobody would show up. I think that continues to be my greatest fear. You spend your entire year planning an event and your greatest fear is that after spending all that on this small festival time-window, the people aren't going to show up. And it's crushing when they don't.

There's always going to be programming mistakes—putting a film in the wrong slot, misjudging your audience's interest in a film—but I found that eventually my audience trusted me and showed up. Most of my screenings have strong audiences now. I'll always worry about audience numbers, and there are still always going to be some heartbreaking moments when the people don't show, but it's just part of the game.

What was your biggest surprise during that first event?

I guess a couple of things. Everything was way harder than it needed to be. Members of the venue's staff were surprisingly difficult to work with (despite initially being seen as partners rather than just a venue we were renting); they were sort of resistant to everything. In retrospect, thinking about how new the arthouse cinema was on the scene, I think it was really about them not knowing what they were doing.

What I mean by making things difficult is: you know when you're working with a company and you're paying them and then they treat you like a customer because you're paying them? That's the way it's supposed to work. But that didn't happen; the dynamic was backwards. Despite my paying them for the use of the venue, they acted like they were doing me a favor. They also had their noses bent out of joint because they thought they would get to program the films. It was a surprise because the director of that theater at the time seemed to really welcome the festival. It was weird: I kind of had to prove myself to them. But in time it got better.

Another surprise during that first planning year, and something I laugh about now, is that when the Dean contacted me, he had already assembled a board. The festival wasn't a non-profit at that point, and although there were a few really helpful, supportive people on the board, there were also a bunch of people who I didn't even know why they were on it. This was a surprise. I essentially inherited a fundamentally disinterested board (with notable exceptions, of course). The legacy of that was something I had to contend with for years. And I didn't have the confidence at the time to disinvite them from the board. I wouldn't let that happen these days. Live and learn.

Another surprise at the time (although not now) was that people's (and by people I mean board members, committee members, the venue director, and others) primary interest in being involved in the festival was to "pick the movies." So, when I (naturally) didn't let these people program films, when they suggested that I program some five-year-old foreign film about an obscure topic and I didn't program it, they were pissed. They were angry with me that I didn't let them program the festival. So, that was a little bit of a surprise and that was something that I learned to manage better as I went along.

So, you inherited a board before you were a non-profit. Are you a non-profit now?

No, the festival never became a non-profit, which I think was ultimately something that has made it very difficult. It was always a project at the university, but not financially supported by the university. I could use the university's non-profit status for grant writing for fundraising, and could accept tax-deductible gifts. They also provided some accounting and financial oversight, and I had office space. So there was some support in there, but it was a sort of strange experience to be commissioned to do something without financial support beyond the first few months.

As for the board, the first thing I did was schedule a meeting. That was a challenge because only about half of the board members were local. Of the 17 members, two attended. From that point I knew that having a traditional board meeting format was not going to work. If this were to happen today, we would have video chat board meetings, but this was in 2008 and the landscape was a bit different than it is today. And really they just weren't that interested; even the local folks didn't show up to that first meeting. In fact, many of those people didn't even attend the festival. Crazy, now that I think about it.

Ultimately I identified the key board members and maintained relationships with them—I called them periodically for advice. Some of them never really engaged, but I did my best. And I had a few gems in there and I've always been grateful for those folks.

So, you're still not a non-profit, but you're using a fiscal sponsor.

Exactly, and I think that that ultimately has made the festival very vulnerable. At the end of the day, I'm mixed about whether the association with the university was an asset or a liability. There are some resources that I had access to, but there are a lot of limitations I had to work under, very strict limitations on who I could approach for money. So, I think in a lot of ways it handicapped me. Had I incorporated as a non-profit, which is something that could still happen, I would absolutely approach those big sponsors as well as foundations that were off-limits to me due to the university already having a relationship with them.

From where I stand now, I think incorporating as a non-profit makes sense. It would have cost me a lot more work at the time, which I didn't have. Because on top of everything I had to do for the festival, the notion of adding "run a non-profit" to that list wasn't very appealing. The bit of support from the university that gave me fiscal sponsorship and financial oversight was enough for me at that point.

I think that if I were to re-energize around this festival the first thing I would do is establish it as a non-profit. I'm not even sure where it's going to go from here. The question of ownership about the film festival is actually something that keeps me up at night, because in a lot of ways the festival was founded and shaped by me, and I don't want to see someone undo the hard work I put into creating it. And ultimately it was a fantastic festival that my community loved. Filmmakers told me I was doing something really special, and I think I was. I need to take a break from it, yet I created it and there isn't really anyone to fill my shoes. Despite the relationship with the university, it's sort of tricky—the question of ownership of the festival might come into play. We'll see what happens. Everyone's on good terms and I'm sure something good will develop if the will is there.

Talk about your hiatus.

Like so many of these people who run film festivals, I felt like every year I was pushing a rock uphill. And that rock never got lighter. I never felt professionally settled in because everything—my salary, whether I would do the festival next year, etc.—was always on the line. My institution didn't support me in a way that I needed them to, never advocated for the festival to be prioritized at the university. An outside consultant did a communications strategic plan for my department at the university and told them that from an outreach perspective, the film festival was absolutely the most important thing they were doing. And they still didn't formalize my role or provide additional support. And I realized that I was playing a part in that unhealthy dynamic by implicitly agreeing to participate in it. And I needed to get away. It would be easy to say that it was time for me to split from the university and become a non-profit, but by then I was truly burned out and that question of ownership was dicey. I still maintain the website and a very small social media presence; the audience is still there. I've done some one-off events with great success, so I'm not completely out of it. But I'm enough out of it to not feel oppressed by it anymore.

A few months after I decided to take the hiatus, I started a full-time position at the university for a professor who works on the Gulf oil spill. The grant I'm working under is well funded, and for the first time in years, I have a decent salary and benefits. No wonder I was kind of a wreck for seven years while I did the festival. Not knowing if I could pay myself and having to beg for money all the time is pretty soul-crushing. Or at least it was for me. No wonder I felt so professionally unsecure: I was.

So, about the hiatus. In the spring of 2014, I did the sixth festival, which was fantastic. Every festival without a doubt was better than the last. I had already made the decision to take a break before that festival happened. But I knew that this was part of the roller coaster of doing a film festival; at some point during each year I decided I was going to be done after the next festival, then the festival would happen and it turned out great so I ditched my plans to leave and jumped back onto it like an addict. But after that 2014 festival I realized I'm going to go crazy. I think a lot of festival directors have that schizophrenia about our festivals; a lot of us are always a few minutes away from saying we're done with this. I decided after that last festival that I needed to take a break.

I don't know what my next step is, but I feel pretty sure that directing and programming EcoFocus Film Festival by myself is not in my future. I absolutely love film and am totally convinced that film, and watching films with other people, is inspiring and can change the world. I want to stay in that world. I don't see my current job as my forever job, but I have already found a couple of opportunities to combine my love of film with my current position. I might bring EcoFocus back, but a certain set of conditions will have tobe present (even if I have to bring those conditions into being), including forming a team.

Do you consider yourself a perfectionist?

Totally. Don't you think a lot of film festival organizers are, though? I think we are the pickiest people possible. It's why we film festival organizers aren't even capable of attending a conference or event and totally enjoying it—we're picking it apart and trying to figure out how to make it better. I'm a super critical person; if you want my honest opinion I'll tell you (hopefully with kindness). In a lot of ways managing a film festival is great for a perfectionist, because there are so many details and a true desire to produce something wonderful.

How do you define success?

That's a good question.

It doesn't have to be about the festival. It could be success in general.

In general, I think success is having a life where you feel you're making a contribution to your community or your field. For me success would also include a good fit between my skills and the work, and being valued for that. This is a tall order, but I'd also like to get some joy out of my work. It's a lot of hours of our lives, and it can't be all Sturm und Drang all the time. Laughter must be involved; it's been my savior.

I think, at the end of the day, the most important thing in my life is my family. I used to think I was kind of workaholic, but I'm now exposed to people who really are sacrificing their families, their health, their relationships, and their happiness for their work. I don't think I was a workaholic at all; I'm just really dedicated to what I do. Now I realize that you can be passionate and dedicated without being a workaholic. I want to be someone who has a pretty healthy work/life balance and takes care of my family, my relationships and myself. I don't want to have regrets. That, to me is success.

Where do you see the event in three to five years?

I think because it's in such a limbo right now, there are a lot of different ways that it could go, many of which I think I'd be pretty happy about.

I think that EcoFocus could morph really nicely into a year-round environmental film series and be just as successful. Anytime I do one-offs, and I've done a couple since starting my hiatus, they've sold out because it's a nice way for people to consume these films without feeling overwhelmed. So, the future of the festival could be something like that.

In order for EcoFocus to ever resume in the way that it was before, I would need to have a small team of people who are as invested in it as I am, which is something that I was never able to make happen, but it still could, and with a fresh start one day I feel like I would know how to build that.

I don't know what it's going to look like in three to five years, but I've also decided that it's okay if it doesn't happen. It's a shame, but I need to just be okay with that. I need to be able to look back at six awesome festivals and say that was great. The idea that I did the film festival by myself for that long is pretty crazy, but pretty amazing, really. It's okay to step away from it.

I am trying to stay on top of new developments with festivals, films, and specifically environmental films. I work for Sundance during the festival each year, and I will continue that even now. I want to make sure that I stay fresh so that if an opportunity comes up, I can dive in. I also just love this stuff, so it's not like this is hard for me to do. I think that programming the festival for my community is a real skill that I've developed, and I hope it will set me up for something film or film festival related in the future. And EcoFocus could be part of that.

You felt the need to go to Sundance because it's an important part of who you are.

I brought up Sundance because by attending Sundance and seeing the documentaries that premiere there, I might be able to facilitate bringing those films to my community. I'm on the board of our arthouse cinema and have a good relationship with their new director. It's eight years old now, but it's still really risky for them to program documentaries, much less eco-docs. Perhaps I could figure out a way to work with them to support doc screenings. Keeping track of new films by attending Sundance and other fests could help with that.

As far as Sundance being an important part of who I am: I don't know. Yeah, I guess it is. It's important for me to stay in the game, and if going to Sundance helps me with that right now, then great. And it's fun, of course; it's Sundance and I love the spirit of that festival.

What challenges do you see for the future of film festivals in general?

I think that the big challenge is to engage with and communicate the value of film festivals to audiences and to the filmmakers themselves, while working within the ever-evolving landscape of online distribution and streaming services. I think we can do this in a way that is realistic and not paranoid. There are some real opportunities if we're creative. I would certainly hate to see film festivals replaced by online stuff exclusively. I don't think that's ever going to happen, especially in places where festival-going and independent film audiences are really established, but the first and biggest challenge that comes to mind is going to be navigating that new online landscape.

What's the second challenge that comes to mind?

I remember when I went to that first IFFS [International Film Festival

Summit], and with the exception probably of you and a very small group of people, I felt that a lot of people, probably fairly, didn't take me seriously because I was just another festival popping up on the landscape. They also didn't think I could do a whole festival on environmental films that didn't make people want to jump off a bridge afterward. But I stuck around and proved that it was possible. And the way I did that was to get super clear on my mission: I knew very clearly what I was trying to accomplish.

I think the challenge is that there are so many festivals in the landscape and every festival really needs to be perfectly clear on its mission and why it exists. Who is it reaching? What type of filmmaker is it serving? Where is its focus? Otherwise we just have a lot of noise and that's not good for the industry or filmmakers.

I think another thing I'm a little bit worried about is the discussion around "best practices" for film festivals. Worried is too strong of word. It's on my mind. I get a little bit nervous when they're talking about "best practices" because I think people who are driving that truck are from certain-sized festivals and I think that creating a "one-size-fits-all" set of best management practices is not really going to work for a lot of people.

At the same time, if there were best practices identified that were focused around protecting film festivals, large and small, that would be good. I'm referring to the legal issues that have come up with our colleagues over the past couple of years.

Final question. What words of wisdom would you have for someone who wants to start a film festival—other than "don't"?

I guess a couple of things. One of them is: you absolutely have to know your audience. And if you don't know them, get to know them. Figure out who what you're doing appeals to.

The second big thing that really helped me turn a corner a couple of years in was developing an understanding for what my festival was and, more importantly, what it wasn't and whose needs I actually didn't have to serve. I got a lot better at responding when someone came to me and said, "I have this great idea; you need to do it," or worse, a criticism that I wasn't doing things the way they thought I ought to. I realized that with a super clear mission statement and vision for the festival, I could process that feedback constructively. This was challenging.

For example, I got criticized for being too focused on the film side and not being "activist enough." But I had decided for good reason that the festival wasn't an activist film festival: I didn't want it to be, and I think it was a stronger film festival because of it. If I got too politicized, I would turn off the very audience I was trying to reach. I focused on film quality, making authentic connections with the filmmakers, providing information and inspiration to my audiences. They could take that inspiration and do whatever they wanted with it, but I couldn't take on the task of also doing community organizing around environmental issues. It took me a couple of years to not feel like I had to take this on. Once I got better at dealing with this and understanding my festival's mission, I could examine someone's feedback or criticism and think about whether it fit with my vision for the festival. That's really important. It's a version of saying no.

I think it's really about knowing who you are and why you want to do this. And be honest! If you are starting a brand new festival: why are you doing it? Is there someone else in your town or region who is also doing it (or something similar)? If so, can you partner with them, help them, suggest an idea and actually be willing to carry it out? What are you actually providing for your community? You know, I'm working in a really small community; when all the students are in town and you count outlying areas, there's 100,000 people around here, maybe 750,000 depending on how far out you go. It would be really weird, then, for somebody else to start a kind of niche film festival that related to my niche film festival. I've seen a bit of that happen, mostly with occasional one-off events, and wonder why they didn't reach out to me—I could have at least helped them build audience for their event. Just don't operate in a vacuum: know what's happening around you and take a really critical look at whether your proposed festival adds to or clutters the landscape. And for god's sake please don't do this because you want a place to show your own or your friends' films, or because you want to meet filmmakers and famous people.

I think it's important is to be really clear on why you're doing what you're doing and to understand the enormity of what you're getting into, because once you do it and your audience likes it, they want more and you're going to kill yourself to give it to them.

ELSA LANKFORD
WAMM Festival

Elsa Lankford is an Associate Professor at Towson University, teaching audio production and post-production classes in the EMF department. In addition to teaching and developing EMF and interdisciplinary classes, Elsa advises EMF students and is the faculty advisor of the Towson Audio Production Society (TAPS). Elsa is the co-founder and chair for the WAMM Festival (Women And Minority in Media Festival) celebrating diversity in media production. Elsa is an interdisciplinary artist who works in multiple media—sound, music, photography, and writing about urban issues, particularly Baltimore City. Elsa has published articles on urban soundscapes, created audio documentaries on urban concerns, such as the Highway to Nowhere in West Baltimore, and has mixed and composed music for films and documentaries.

First, what is your background? What did you do before you started a film festival?

I teach audio in a film and media program, Electronic Media and Film (EMF) at Towson University in Maryland. I am also an interdisciplinary artist, musician, and composer. I've always been very interested in stories and diversity. I have chosen fields of work and study that have been fairly male-dominated fields: audio, computers, and technology.

I co-created WAMM Fest, Women And Minority Media Festival, in 2008 to both celebrate and encourage diversity within the EMF department. It started with a focus on student and local media makers.

Did you have any festival experience before this?

Yes. I created and ran a music/arts festival in Baltimore City for several years, and I was involved with an annual environmental art festival/outdoor installation for several years as well. I had been involved with planning those festivals, and volunteering and attending other film festivals, but I can't say that I had done anything else on this scale.

You mentioned that you wanted to highlight the diversity of your students and your faculty. What else was part of that original mission?

It was to highlight and celebrate diversity in students' projects, and to also give them role models so that they could see what kind of path they could take. The goal was to bring in guest artists who are diverse, and to also bring in younger kids who could be encouraged to see this as something that young women, people of color, and people of any sexuality can create to make their voices heard and their stories told.

It is also hopefully the start of a pipeline to be able to get more diversity on screen—film, video, TV, music production—and to make our department part of that bigger picture.

Did you have an audience in mind when you created this?

When it was first created, it was really for our students, other film and media students of all ages, and professionals in the region. The community was certainly invited, but in the very beginning, it was designed to be a small festival. After I took the helm as director, I became focused on obtaining more of a balance of community and student participants.

How did you choose a programming strategy?

The programming strategy has evolved over the years. We just finished up our eighth year of WAMM Fest. In the beginning—and I can say this because it was true—we were really begging students for entries. We were asking time and time again to get students to enter. So our acceptance rate was very high, because it was so difficult to get entries. The process was also a paper system. We'd have paper entries, and we'd have to go to the different high schools and try to figure out physical collection mechanisms to get these entries there. It was a much different festival when it first started. It was very, very small scale.

Your programming style has changed over the years, obviously.

Probably five years ago, we moved the call for entries online. It was not with one of the central systems, but it was online and we started to get a lot more entries, some of which were international. As soon as we went to the online submission system Withoutabox, we started to get a lot of entries. The more entries we had, the more competitive the entries became and I was able to create a more coherent and comprehensive program.

Programming is probably the hardest, but also the most satisfying, part of running the festival. It's definitely my favorite aspect. It starts after we've done several rounds of elimination, but even while I'm judging some of the beginning entries, I can see that there are certain films that will end up being a final piece of the puzzle.

Programming for a diversity-based festival is going to differ from other kinds of fests, because we want to make sure that stories are told from the perspective of the person we're seeing on the screen. We also want to highlight the talent and skills of women and minorities filmmakers.

Once the films are selected, programming blocks are decided upon, whether thematic or by category. Each film is twenty minutes or less, so we also choose programming around which films will fit together best to give the audience a fulfilling emotional and educational experience. What ends up working can be extremely eclectic. But I think the audience would be surprised to know how much work it takes to get it to this point, and while it is eclectic, if the programming is done well, the pieces work together well.

While a lot of programming happens during the final judging stages, even from the beginning, I am starting to get a sense of how pieces may gel together and work well in the festival and with our audience.

Since you created the festival from scratch, how did that process evolve to how you choose today?

That's a great question, because it's changed so much. I used to be involved with watching and listening to everything—we also have audio entries. We had a lot fewer judges. This past year, we had about one hundred judges, which, for us, is really incredible. I wasn't able to watch all of the entries this year, and honestly, that was a turning point for me.

We've also had over double the entries that we've had in the past. I created an online Google Docs form that requires judges to answer questions about the production value, the story, the technical quality, and the film's inclusion of diversity in all aspects of its creation. I have to evaluate those responses and incorporate those into the final selection process. This requires me to trust the judges to understand the vision of the festival.

Some of the entries are really good, but not right for WAMM. For example, some had women in weak or stereotypical female roles, which is not adding to diversity in media. Ultimately, it's about taking the judges' responses and making sure that these are films that fit within the mission statement for WAMM, and that work in the programming stages too.

Going into your first year, what were some of your greatest fears?

That nobody would show up. Honestly, I think that was probably my greatest fear in the beginning, and that still stands. Am I going to get enough people to experience this? Is the audience going to like it, and what kind of technical problems are going to stop this from happening?

What has been your greatest success or greatest surprise?

The greatest success is probably having a full house. That is a great feeling, no matter how big or small the venue. Each year, it's about achieving that: getting as many people to the festival to experience, learn, discuss, enjoy, and laugh. That's really what all the hard work is about.

But another great success was having 16 of the 54 filmmakers here last year. We've always had a few filmmakers, but never this many. And one of the greatest surprises was to see how well attended and informational the filmmaker's panel was this year. I've never offered that before, but getting these filmmakers to sit and share their experiences with the audience and the other panelists was very powerful.

How do you define success? It doesn't necessarily have to be in context of the festival.

I'm a teacher, so this is where this is coming from: success would be that an idea has gotten through to somebody, that an emotional connection has been made. To me, that is the best: when people either audibly or visibly have gotten something that I'm talking about or that the filmmaker has portrayed. Maybe it was really hard for the audience to see or hear, but they've understood it.

One of the films we showed at WAMM this past year was set in the 1990s, about two guys in high school who seemed to be in a platonic relationship, and when they kissed on screen, the audience broke out in applause. That, to me, was probably one of the best moments of the festival. There was that connection, and it was expressed in a way that just really made me tear up, especially with the filmmaker there.

You're a program at the university. Does your funding come through the university?

Our funding is primarily from the university, which I realize is a luxury that not all festivals have. It's not a lot of money, but it's enough to work with. We also bring in some money from the calls for entry, so that does definitely help. We keep our entry fees very low (this year we actually opened the call for entries with no fees to kick things off), but even so, the entry fees, particularly for students, are extremely reasonable. Our ticket prices are also very low, but that does help a little bit, too.

We used to have free tickets for the festival itself, but I have found that having the tickets with a cost associated with them, even nominal a cost as I feel ours are, is beneficial. But primarily, our money comes from the university, the EMF department where I teach, and the College of Fine Arts and Communications.

You don't have a board, unlike most non-profit festivals, or unlike for-profit festivals which have shareholders or owners with a financial investment. Are there restrictions because you're part of the university or are you given autonomy? How do you balance that?

Currently, I'm given a lot of autonomy. There are definitely restrictions—most of which I have learned by just by doing this for eight years. Since it's not just a university, it's a public university, there are more rules and restrictions than private schools. But on the other hand, I don't need to clear things with a board or shareholders. I won't bore you with the details, but it's very different than a lot of festivals. Knowing what I can and can't expense is always forefront in my decisions for buying anything. Luckily, I work with great people who help me make the financial side work.

Does the university have any say as far as content?

No, they do not. They are not involved with the programming decisions. I've had no problems with that. I have had complete control over the creative side of the festival. That is, again, a good thing about being in the university, especially within an arts college. They would support me no matter what.

Tell me about last year's festival. How many films, audiences, venues?

Last year, we screened 54 shorts in seven screenings over three days with about 700 audience members. For some festivals, that's going to seem like a very small number. We have a fairly small venue, and it's always a challenge to get people to come out to diversity programming.

I've been working a lot on marketing, which is really probably the biggest challenge that I have. The main focus of WAMM is diversity, but that's not how I get most people here. I get people here by having really good films, programming them well, and making the experience a lot of fun.

Let's talk about audience development, because that's a big issue. What do you do to develop your audience? If you had resources, what do you wish you could do?

That's always a big topic for us. Definitely, Facebook. I had an intern for the first time this year and that was really helpful. She did some of the Facebook posts, Twitter, and Instagram messaging. I did a lot of Facebook ads that were targeted to the tri-state area. I made sure to get a lot of printed materials out to any place that would have a potential audience member. On this campus, we had postcards and posters all over, but we also promoted to other universities that have film and media programs and/or gender programs, like Women's Studies, Black Studies, African American Studies, LGBT/Queer, Latino, etc.

We use Eventbrite for tickets. As soon as people buy tickets, they get on our mailing list and we make sure that we're messaging people that the festival is coming up. Word of mouth, honestly, is probably the biggest asset. Part of our other challenge is that we're on a campus. Getting people to a campus for an event is sometimes more challenging than it should be, because of parking restrictions or the feeling that a college campus is not a traditional festival venue.

There's so much I wish I could do, more social media, more events, more help. I wish I could get more well-known film and media makers here throughout the year, and to have events that would help grow and build audiences. I'd like to have more programming in the community. I'd love to work more with K-12 schools and after school programs to show how powerful and fun film and media making can be, and to try to encourage young students to get involved.

Do you sell an all-access pass as an audience cultivation tool?

This year, we only sold individual tickets. However, we've sold passes in the past, and I loved the idea of it, and I still love the idea of it. I thought that it would encourage people to go to more screenings, and it did. But with limited staffing, it made it hard to count and track usage. You didn't know each time a passholder would go to a screening, so it made it very difficult to predict if a screening would sell out or not.

You have one hundred reviewers. That is a huge number, as some festivals have five, others a dozen. I thought DC Shorts was unique with eighty. How do you develop relationships with those reviewers? How have you have built the review process so that you can trust their decisions?

First, there has to be trust. I'd say that the number of judges increased this year by about twenty people. That means that there are seventy or so who have worked with me in the past, so we all know what to expect. I have a core group of about seven people that I trust implicitly that have worked for the festival multiple years, and are part of my "advisory board." I totally trust their judging opinion.

Our call for entries last year ran from August to the end of December. I probably had about fifty judges in the beginning of the semester, one hundred by the end. Most of those new judges came in at once towards the end of our regular judging. It was really, really difficult. Those fifty new people came in over the course of probably a week. I was trying to get across the ideas of the festival. I changed the online judging form to make sure the objectives of the festival were clear. This judging form is crucial to the process, and even when I can't look at all the films, I look at all the judging comments, not just the scores, to make sure that a film doesn't slip through the cracks.

Because we are an academic festival, the call starts in the summer and runs through the fall semester, with a deadline at the end of October. I also have certain judges pre-screening, so that stronger films will go to most of the judges. This year, films that make it into Official Selections will probably have ended up going through four rounds of judging. And that's necessary since in 2015 we have received over 1,000 entries for probably fifty spots.

You are managing the festival at the same time you're teaching. The festival's a big commitment, even with only seven screenings; it's still a year's worth of planning. How do you juggle that?

Because I teach college, I'm off contract over the summer. I'm still doing other things for work, but I do usually have some time to help get the process started. I try to balance out my teaching schedule with my festival schedule. It's definitely a lot of work; the key is finding ways to tie it into other aspects of my teaching and workload, which now, nine years in, I'm still working on. I cancel classes for the week of the festival; that's stated in the syllabus. That way, I definitely have time for that last minute stuff that comes up.

This year, as I did a few years ago, I'm going to have a class for WAMM Fest. These students will help work on the festival and find out what it really takes to make a festival happen.

When I say it's seven screenings, it really sounds like it's so small, but it is so much work. If people knew how much work was involved…I don't know. Maybe they'd run for the hills.

What are some of the additional programs you've implemented over the years that have been successful—and maybe some that have not been? What have you learned from that?

We always have a master class. I'd love to do more, because we are a festival at a university. I don't just want people to be learning through these stories on film. I want filmmakers and potential film and media makers to be able to learn more about their craft as well. We've been really lucky with some of the guest artists that we've been able to present. Given our budget, we're definitely limited on who we can bring in.

This year, I experimented. In the past, the guest artist has taught a master class and then on the last night of the festival, we've screened their film. Whether they're giving a talk or whether they're screening a film that was always a challenge, marketing-wise, to screen these short films for two of the nights, and then the last night, to switch gears, and say, "here's this film by this filmmaker from Hollywood."

As much as I love the idea of having somebody who found success and could be a role model, it takes a large chunk of time from the schedule. We spend so much time reviewing submissions and asking filmmakers to send in their films, that to take a few hours out of a crowded weekend to showcase one person is not always in line with our mission. I think that we can, and should, have more master classes throughout the year, but the festival is about the submissions.

What was also a great success this year was having travel money for filmmakers. We were able to bring in 16 filmmakers from all over the country. We even had a filmmaker from Turkey, so that was awesome. To be able to have more filmmakers than we've ever had, the most films we've ever played: I loved being able to do that. It was fun to be able to screen a film, have the filmmakers see the audience response, and then during the break allow the audience to interact with the filmmakers. I just think that's a win-win for everybody.

What are some of the biggest challenges facing the festival today?

Funding, of course. And venues. Our venue has an awesome screen and an awesome projector for a great picture. It just doesn't have enough seats. That's a good problem to have, but trying to figure out where it's going to move has been a challenge. Can it be off campus? Can it be in the city? That, to me, is probably the main thing.

Then growth. How to get more programming without stretching myself too thin? How can this get bigger? How do I get more people to help? I'm working on that. I need to find and cultivate volunteers who can do this for the love of it until we can figure out how to start paying people—which may never be possible.

In what ways has the festival exceeded your original vision?

As soon as we got the call on Withoutabox, our bar was raised so much higher. We really saw a massive increase in the number and quality of films.

This past year we had 19 countries represented by the films. Having these really strong international entries is really inspirational. Now with the call on both Withoutabox and Film Freeway, starting with a free entry period, we have over 1,000 entries from over 75 countries, but also from the university and from the Baltimore area. That is truly mind-blowing.

Looking back, would you have changed anything from the start?

No, I actually don't think I would have. At first, I was going to say that maybe I would have liked to have access to something like Withoutabox, an online submission engine, earlier, but I don't think that our system or I could have handled it. At that point, it was still a committee working on the festival. It needed to start really small and local, and grow organically. I think that was how this needed to happen.

Where do you see WAMM Fest in three to five years?

I'd really like to do more year-round programming. I'd also love to be able to take WAMM on the road to some different places. I think that it could definitely play other places, and it would be really cool to be able to do that.

I'd like to see more female and minority filmmakers and not just on film, but TV and trans media. Hopefully, WAMM is something that won't need to exist at some point when media and film becomes diverse, but that's going to be, unfortunately, a long time.

And of course, I want to see bigger audiences and stronger films, but also getting more local films, too. There's so much that we can do with younger kids to get them to realize that this is a way that they can get their stories told and get their voices heard. This is not just for straight white men. It's really for everybody, and the more diverse the voices, the better everything is.

What are you most proud of, or what do you hope would have been your biggest impact for the future of your festival?

There has to be more diverse media. Whether that is just here at the university, where we get more diverse students making more diverse media. Or some high school kid decides to come to Towson to do this program because they want to be a filmmaker to get their story told, or WAMM gives a woman or minority filmmaker the encouragement to continue and an opportunity to screen their work, I think that increasing diversity can be the best impact that this festival could make and that I could make. That's my goal with it, and that is the best thing that could happen.

What challenges do you see for the future of film festivals?

Because I get short films, I get a subset of films that other festivals would get. I may not be seeing all the same challenges that other festivals have. We do get some of our money from the call for entries, and I try to keep our entry fees low, but at some point, I'm wondering if that's sustainable. If we are charging money for people to enter their films, are they going to still enter them?

I agree with you. At some point, using festivals as a distribution platform might backfire economically. If you're spending $1,000 entering film festivals, you're better off taking that money and spending it on an online distributor and online marketing.

More people may see the film. But, you don't get the laurels or credit for playing in front of a live audience.

Yeah, you said it much better than I did, but yes!

Last question: what are some words of wisdom for someone who wants to start a film festival?

My initial thought is don't do it. Volunteer with an existing festival first to learn and understand the commitment you really have to make. You have to be super dedicated. If you go to a festival, and you think how awesome that festival is, that has probably taken somebody just an enormous amount of time. The question to ask yourself is: do you have time to do this? I'm coming from a specific background of being at a university, but when I did run a festival on my own, it wasn't so much the money, it was the time. Do you have people in your life who will put up with you as you're working on this festival and maybe continuously talking about the festival?

It's making sure what your priorities are, making sure about your time. I can't stress it enough how much time it takes up, and possibly sanity as well.

DAN BRAWLEY
Cucalorous Film Festival

Dan Brawley has worked for over 17 years in the film industry as the Executive Director of the Cucalorus Film Festival. Experienced in community organizing, event planning and collaboration, Dan is a self-identifying ceremonialist with a habit for artistic entrepreneurship and experimentation. In other words, he is a cool guy with mad skills.

Before you were with Cucalorus, what did you do? What is your background?

I was at Duke University in 1994 when Cucalorus started. I moved back to Wilmington, NC to work in the film industry, and got a job working on *The Adventures of Elmo in Grouchland*, and *Muppets in Space*, as a welder. I was doing a lot of sculpture, a little bit of performance art. It was there that I met some key Twinkle Dooners, the crew that started Cucalorus, so I got looped in in 1997. I joke about the way I got my job: I kept showing up to the office, and one day, I was the only guy there. Someone called and asked who was in charge and I said I was. So that's how I got my job: by showing up.

Cucalorus is la high-risk sort of venture, an entrepreneurial business. For the first six or so years, it was really a front porch endeavor: You guys bring the beer, we'll bring the projector. Filmmakers were not desperate, but certainly eager to share their work. There was camaraderie, a certain understanding between the filmmakers, and those of us who were running the festival. We were all the same little community of people supporting each other.

It was really after the fifth or sixth festival, that I thought, "OK, this is going somewhere. We need to start building a foundation underneath the house."

What was the impetus to start the event?

Wilmington was unique in that the studio that Dino DeLaurentiis built in the mid '80s brought a lot of resources to town that weren't available elsewhere. There was an emerging indie scene in Wilmington, where people were borrowing equipment from big-budget productions.

So filmmakers started using the tail ends that weren't being used on those shows, and really leveraging all the leftover resources from bigger shows to make shorts and develop their own projects. Cucalorus was an excuse to come together and share work with each other. It was really simple. It's been non-competitive from the very beginning; it was really important that the festival not give out any awards. That creates an atmosphere that is very relaxed, almost like an artist's retreat, where you're just getting together with your friends to share and talk about the work that's being made.

When the event was created, was there an intended audience, or was it just anyone who loved film?

I don't know if it was intentional or not. Because of what was happening in Wilmington in the early 1990s, there were a lot of filmmakers in the audience. Empire Records was being shot in Wilmington when the first festival was held, so Liv Tyler and Renée Zellweger attended.

That is very cool.

It's kind of natural. A lot of the things we've done have been less intentional and more organic. It's been a process of discovery. As opposed to a committee of people getting together and setting up some strategy, our process has been a little bit more like Our Gang: "Let's climb up into the tree house and have some fun." Only maybe later considering, "Oh, wait, this is what we're doing."

So you came on board to codify what was being done and implement procedures and systems. What was that like?

It was a great fit, for me. I was spending half my time in the studio, making sculptures and experimenting as an artist. I had studied art history at Duke. I was naturally drawn to be an organizer. It ended up being a really good fit for my skills.

I think one of the great things for me is that over the last 17 years I've actually learned my job while doing my job. I don't think a lot of people get a chance to do that. I didn't know what I was doing. I was in my early twenties, and all of a sudden I was running a film festival. We made some funny mistakes along the way that we learned from.

I grew up in Wilmington, so I was able to pull together some resources to help grow the festival that other people wouldn't have had access to.

What was your budget during those early years?

Gosh. I think we had a couple thousand dollars in the bank. Maybe by the fifth year, we might have had $10,000 in cash.

That is really scraping it together.

Yeah, totally. I think the filmmakers who were coming to the festival could relate to that, because they were in the same boat. They were making short films, even features, with really small budgets. When they stepped into the Cucalorus world, they could relate to the scrappy attitude that we brought to it.

Is the budget still small?

I would say no. Our cash budget is between $300,000 and $400,000. When you include the in-kind donations, we get up to about twice that much.

We just did an analysis and found that our budget has grown, on average, about 23 percent a year. That's not going to continue. I mean it would be cool if it did. When you start at zero, it's easy to have some impressive numbers like that.

Can you talk about your path to become a non-profit organization? Were there any roadblocks?

I have some complicated feelings about the non-profit industry, and how it relates to artistic endeavors. The 501(c)(3) model is really borrowed from philanthropic foundations, and in my mind, is the complete opposite of what an artist-driven, visionary movement needs to succeed. But when you are a small arts organization in a small town, it's important.

We became a non-profit organization because it was the doorway to grants and donations. Somewhere in the ballpark of fifty to eighty percent of what I do, I consider to be just pure entrepreneurship. In some ways, arts endeavors are super-high risk. There's no reward at the end. It's almost the purest form of entrepreneurship, where it's all risk, no reward. You just have some people who are really passionate about what they're doing.

Describe your first board as a non-profit. How did you find them?

Our board started with the people who were in the room. Everybody who was involved was really passionate about this precious thing that we had started, which, even in the early days, had some sort of mystical quality to it. We weren't letting just anybody in the room. You had to go through hell, through the fire, to be sitting at the table. Obviously, years later, that's changed a lot. Our board is now representative of the community: business leaders, people from the film industry, and alumni filmmakers.

In the early days, we had a lot of founders in the room. There was a lot of wrestling with how to balance the distinct qualities that make Cucalorus special with the need to provide a greater service to filmmakers, contribute to the evolution of film festivals, and to the evolution of filmmaking.

Founder's Syndrome is a big issue for many organizations. Some founders are great and get out of the way, and others do not. Did you have some of those issues?

There have been some uncomfortable moments. I just put my head down and worked my ass off, and just tried to plow through. I hold the vision of the festival deep inside of me. I just need to rely on that vision.

Luckily, we've got a strong core group of people, many of them founders, who have stuck with this festival. Matt Malloy, the Emcee for the festival, is the same guy who introduced the very first screening in 1994. There are always a couple of founders on the board. They are open minded and excited to see the festival change and grow over the years. We've been really lucky in a lot of ways that connection to our founding has never really been lost. That consistency is, I think, a little bit rare.

What are some of the biggest challenges that you face?

Film festivals have to be really adaptable, especially in an environment that is arguably over saturated. There are dozens of film festivals in Wilmington, and we are a smallish coastal city in North Carolina.

There are thousands of film festivals in the world. It seems like such an incredibly popular thing to do right now. How do you deal with what could be seen as competition? I choose to see it as really helping me: I see every event as helping with audience cultivation. One city wouldn't need just one restaurant, so why would any city need just one film festival? I'm delighted to see film festivals popping up. I think it's an exciting space for experimentation, and testing out new ideas.

Running a festival can be difficult when you're not well-defined. One of the things that the explosion of film festivals has forced us to do is to be much more specific about what we're looking for, who we are, and how we connect with filmmakers. That competition has really driven Cucalorus to be better.

I also think there are challenges with how to deal with online distribution. How do you deal with so much stuff streaming? I don't really get caught up in that, because I think there's a quality to sitting in a dark room with a bunch of people that's so powerful. We're not rewriting our game plan just yet, in that regard.

I think funding is always an issue. In the cultural funding world, film festivals are still relatively new, and maybe still misunderstood. The major cultural funders, in my mind, are still stuck in the twentieth century mindset. In the long view, I don't think there's anything to worry about. Film festivals have become one of the more dominant cultural gathering points. When you look at the long view, film festivals sit at a pretty sweet spot.

Can you talk about Cucalorus' initial programming strategy? How has that evolved?

When I walked into the door in the nineties, there were so many filmmakers who were dying to reach any audience, who thought, "No way, you guys are going to bring a hundred people into a bar to see my movie. This is the coolest thing ever." Now, twenty years later, it's a little bit more complicated. We've had to adapt and become more specific about what we're doing.

We've found that navigating a film festival can be a really challenging for the audience. When I travel to other festivals, I spend a lot of time reading the program guide, and trying to map out my strategy.

I've tried to create a way for audiences to get an idea of what they're getting into before they grab a ticket and get a seat. Our programming strings are hopefully an aid, a guide for audience members.

Cucalorus has a variety of programming strings including Magnolia for films that have won awards on the festival circuit and are a little more high-profile, Vanguard for emerging talent, with a recent focus on female directors, and we have a social justice program called Voices.

How do you handle film submissions?

I think every festival has to pick their own strategy, and has to decide how they want to handle that.

It is still really valuable to put out a call for entries. Sit back in your office, and wait for films to come in. You dig through them. You spend hours and hours and hours, digging. You discover that "one," and, holy shit—this is it, right?

But for us, that approach isn't enough. I'm not just going to sit back and wait for filmmakers to come to me. I'm also really aggressively out there, attending festivals all over the country, all over the world. I am looking for films that aren't going to show up in my mailbox. I take advice from alumni who might be attending festivals that I can't get to. Also being really curious, I'm looking for filmmakers who are sometimes too busy to send their film to a hundred different festivals.

How do you cultivate and develop your audience?

We do events throughout the year in Jengo's Playhouse, our community cinema. We run other, little festivals, including fun one-offs. A few years ago, we had a Cheese Sandwich Film Festival that was launched by a young staffer named Joselyn McDonald who believed that there was a festival for everything. She was right. We followed that up with a Chips and Salsa Film Festival and then last year the Cough Syrup Film Festival. Who knows what's next?

We do outreach into schools, book clubs, churches, anywhere there are people. Just saying, "Hey, we're doing a movie over here" is not enough. If you really want to connect with people, you have to meet them halfway. Once you've hooked somebody, and you're doing really thoughtful programming, those relationships can sometimes last a very long time.

Have you seen your audience change as the event has matured?

That's a really good question. We're always thinking about how many people are coming. That's what everybody wants to know: What's the number? Sometimes, what the audience looks like is more important than the number. Are they getting older? Younger? More people from out of town? To me, that is important information.

Film festivals have become more mainstream. Ten to fifteen year ago, festivals were for people who were really adventurous, who weren't afraid to take a risk and spend a couple hours in a dark room watching something really weird. Today, people who would once have been a little apprehensive are now diving into it, attending five or six screenings. Maybe that goes hand in hand with the fact that the content that's hitting the screen is also a little more mainstream now. Festivals are not quite as foreign as they were twenty years ago.

How do you develop relationships with sponsors or patrons?

To me, the best place to start is with the event and the content. In the ideal situation, they have had some kind of experience with your festival, or with one of the films. But even if they have not, it's about some common connection that you make. It's all about asking questions, finding out what their interests are. You introduce them to the really cool things that will happen. And you get them hooked. I sound like a drug dealer.

That common ground is key. It is a place where all the interests align, and where there might be an opportunity to work together. I think the one mistake that I see people making is just having one target. Putting all your eggs in one basket is never a good plan.

And I think it's all about genuine relationships: it's all about getting to know people on more than a superficial level. Those connections endure.

At what point did the event become full-time for you?

About nine years ago. It's been a really nice, slow transition. With the way Cucalorus has evolved, there hasn't been one year where we just changed everything and it became a big business. Instead, it has slowly grown over the years.

I don't know if I was even aware that it was becoming a full-time job when that was happening. I love what I do. I love working with filmmakers. I love traveling to other film festivals. I have fallen in love with a handful of cities all over the world because I went there for their film festivals.

Looking back, what are some aspects of the festival that you would have changed?

I don't think about that too often. I have a hard time thinking backward. That's a good question. I'll be thinking about that.

OK. Think about it. How do you define success?

When I'm at the festival and hiding in the shadows, watching what's happening, the thing that really hits my heart is watching people connect with each other. Whether it's a filmmaker with an audience member, or a filmmaker meeting an actor for the first time. Like when Stephen Cone met Josephine Decker at Cucalorus. That just makes me feel good, knowing that the creative energy of those two will come together to create something new. Success is when filmmakers are inspired, or when somebody in the audience is inspired to take a risk and maybe make a film.

When I think about the festival, I think of curating the people who come together. The films are important, obviously, but for me, the people are even more important. In creating the experiences, it's like putting a guest list together for a wild cocktail party. I think about who we are bringing together. The great thing about a film festival, a five-day event with thousands of people, is that you're not actually anticipating all the things that'll happen.

All these happy accidents can happen between screenings, sitting in the filmmaker's lounge or in the backyard by the bonfire. These really special connections happen that live outside of the festival. They live on for years and years. People might meet at Cucalorus, and make a film together three years later. Those are the moments that are really rewarding for me.

I know you're not leaving anytime soon, but do you see yourself doing this indefinitely? Do you see an exit? Are there other interests you want to pursue?

That's one of the cool things about being a part of Cucalorus: it has a life energy that is really beyond any one person. I'm sure the festival embodies a lot of things about me, but there are other people that are just as passionate as I am. They might not spend as many hours per week doing the dirty work but they show up when it matters.

I do think of what else might happen as my role here changes. There are times where I feel like I'm not qualified to do my own job! That's a really cool place to be. We're getting ready to do a national search for a managing director, someone who will run the business in a way that I can't.

I'm keeping myself busy, even beyond the day-to-day of Cucalorus. I imagine when I do leave, that it won't be a big deal. It won't be a big break in the history of Cucalorus. It'll be seamless and organic, just the same way as the festival's growth and evolution has been.

I sometimes think that maybe I've stayed here too long. But even after 17 years, the challenges are different every day. Issues pop up that you never could have dreamed of. That keeps it exciting, and it keeps me engaged.

It's an exciting time for film festivals. With the formation of the Film Festival Alliance and new conferences for festival organizers, I feel really lucky to be part of this world at this particular moment. I think we're going have a great impact on what film festivals look like twenty, thirty, even forty years from now. It's a pretty cool place to be.

I would agree with you. What challenges do you see for the future of film festivals?

I think festivals have to continue to be specific and distinct. I especially like the world that you and I operate in. Obviously, the big-city, star-driven red carpet spectacles operate in a different paradigm. Those of us who are more community-focused have to work hard to be specific and distinct. We have to succinctly articulate exactly what we are doing in a way that's meaningful.

In 1994, it was really meaningful to say we show independent films. Today, I don't know how meaningful that is. I think this forces programmers, curators, festivals, and cinemas, to connect with audiences in more direct ways. We need to be more specific about who we want reach, and how we make that happen. I think with the changing funding and political landscape, its critical to run a tight ship. We should be looking to start-ups and tech companies about being flexible and adaptable. In a field that literally changes every day, you have to be prepared, while not getting distracted by the details.

That's not an easy thing to do—not being distracted or consumed by the next thing that you think is going to happen. Where do you see Cucalorus in ten years?

We recently started a residency program. We have three historic houses behind Jengo's Playhouse, and we are exploring how that folds into the festival's year-round work. We're on the path toward finding out how film festivals can develop even deeper relationships with filmmakers. I realize that Sundance and Tribeca both have major programs to develop filmmakers. But for a community festival like Cucalorus, how can we connect with filmmakers and be a meaningful collaborator on new projects? We're doing something that's exciting and maybe a little bit different. This summer, Jackie Olive is coming for three months to work on a new documentary about the history of lynching in the South.

I'm interested to see what role a film festival can play. How can we turn the film festival model inside out and upside down? How can we further explore the relationship between filmmakers and film festivals? Maybe it is beyond exhibition, and digging into production. Can we encourage filmmakers to start thinking about audiences earlier in the process, and how does that change the way they make films? I think there's a whole rich area that Cucalorus is on the verge of exploring in a meaningful way.

In ten years I'm going be in the backyard of Jengo's Playhouse, standing beside a bonfire, meeting a young filmmaker who's doing crazy stuff with cameras and throwing it on the screen. To me, that's enough. I don't think you always have to grow. I don't think everything has to get bigger. If we can keep connecting with challenging new artists, giving them a place to share their work, that's still very valuable—especially if you do it well.

Last question. What words of wisdom do you have for someone who wants to start a film festival?

I would say, "Hell, yes!" Do it tomorrow. Don't start too big. Start at a manageable scale. Do something meaningful. There's nothing better than a packed house. I don't care how big it is. I don't care if it's your house and there's six people in the living room, or if it's the largest venue in New York City. Nothing feels better than a room packed full of people. Find the filmmakers who live in your ecosystem. Learn as you go along; you don't have to be too careful. That's what I've done, just sort of charge forward. Every once in a while, stop. Look back and pick up the pieces.

Go to other film festivals. That's absolutely essential. Visit six, seven, eight film festivals. Jump in your car and drive to the next city, where there's a festival. Do whatever you can to sit yourself down at a couple of film festivals and watch what they're doing in front of the screen, behind the screen, at the box office. Don't reinvent the wheel, just look at what they're doing and see if you can borrow the good ideas that might work in your community. And go for it!

TERRY SCERBAK
Reel Shorts Film Festival

Terry Scerbak is the founder and Director/Programmer of the Reel Shorts Film Festival in Grande Prairie, a city of 68,000 in northwest Alberta. Her background as a playwright led her to write and produce a short film that screened at the 2006 Edmonton International Film Festival where she was inspired to start a film festival that would bring the world's best short films to Grande Prairie, the first step in her goal of developing a filmmaking community in the region. Terry has been a panelist at the AMAAS (Alberta Media Arts Alliance Society) Conference, the Independent Film Festival Un-Conference, and the International Film Festival Programmers at the Palm Springs International ShortFest.

Since this interview, and after nine years as a program of the Grand Prairie Live Theater Society. representatives from Reel Shorts have agreed to form the festival as its own non-profit society.

Before you started the Reel Shorts Film Festival, what was your background?

I grew up in Edmonton and studied English in university. After moving to Grande Prairie in 1996, I started writing poems, short stories, and plays. I was asked by a couple of people to write a script for a TV pilot. The idea was too similar to a new show that was already on the air so I suggested doing a short film instead. Everyone agreed but then the original producers moved away, so I ended up not only writing it but also producing it. It had a zero budget. All of us involved, actors and crew, added up to only seven people. But it got into the Edmonton International Film Festival. When I went to the fest, I fell in love with one short film in particular, and saw some others that I really liked. On the four-and-a-half-hour drive back home, I thought to myself, "Wouldn't it be nice if my friends and family could see some of those short films?"

Did you have any other mission other than to show great films?

I had no background doing anything like this. I'm actually a fairly shy person, and certainly not one of those people brimming with boundless confidence. I was the last person in the world you would think would start a film festival.

I had some girlfriends who each had put on terrific events from writer conferences to concerts, and just from seeing them do it, I realized there was no reason that I shouldn't give it a try as well. There's a very entrepreneurial spirit in this region.

Producing that short film was like herding cats, because everybody was a volunteer. One actress ended up working nights. The other actress worked days. It was incredibly frustrating to get everybody together, but when it was finally over, I wanted to do it again. I turned around, and there was absolutely nobody to do it with. The director was a theater person who preferred to be on stage, the camera guy was a high school kid who left to go to college, and the sound man got another job so he was too busy. There was no filmmaking community in Grande Prairie, but there is an incredible amount of talent. We had talent on stage at the community theater. I would see unbelievable actors, directors, fantastic writers, musicians, and visual artists. But there was no filmmaking community. I wondered if a film festival would bring people together, and ultimately help create a filmmaking community so I could make films again. And of course, what happens when your talented young people go away to film school? Because the art form is so collaborative, and we didn't have the resources, they didn't come back. That was the challenge.

Ultimately, Reel Shorts has produced some films. It was very successful at being a catalyst for creating a filmmaking community. Because of an internship project we did in 2012, a filmmakers' cooperative started. We just completed our second Frantic48 competition, which is a collaboration with PRIMAA (Peace Region Independent Media Arts Association), the filmmakers' cooperative. Now there's a filmmaking community. I didn't think it would be possible, but it happened.

I realized that to have a thriving filmmaking community, you needed a film festival, but there also needed to be a film school and a filmmakers' cooperative. The residents of this city and region were quite happy with their lives before the festival started. If you'd asked them, "Do we need a short film festival?" nobody would have said yes. But I knew we needed it as the first step to creating a filmmaking community.

Talk a little bit about the community. Grande Prairie is rather isolated.

It's a city of 68,000, the biggest city in a huge geographical area of northwest Alberta and northeast British Columbia. Edmonton is the nearest large city and it's a four-and-a-half-hour drive away. We are the center of a huge region, so we have many more amenities than one would think for a city our size.

I was talking to a young person in Edmonton recently. She used to live in Grande Prairie and I asked her what she enjoyed about being in the big city. She said, "all of the cultural opportunities." So I got to thinking about what the real difference is between a city like Grande Prairie and a much larger city like Edmonton. In Edmonton there are greater opportunities to consume art and culture, but the opportunity to actually create and participate in art is much higher here. Because if you don't have it, you create it. In Edmonton, everything is professional or amateur, whereas here, people don't even make the distinction. Sometimes, people get paid as professionals, and other times, they donate their talents and contribute as part of a community effort to put on a play or a concert or make a film or whatever. Who's the professional and who's the amateur? It's more about how good you are and the opportunity to develop and share that talent.

How long did it take you to plan the first year's event?

It was on the way back from the Edmonton International Film Festival that I had the idea to start the festival and that was in October 2006. If I had stopped for a minute and realized I would have to speak in public, I don't think I ever would have started the festival because that would have terrified me.

I spoke with the manager of Grande Prairie Live Theater because I had volunteered there before. I offered to start and organize a short film festival, and she responded, "Great!" That was the whole process. It's a great place to start something new. Nobody asks you, "What are your qualifications?" or gives you all the reasons why it won't work. You're just given the opportunity to do it.

Two weeks later, there was an Art of the Peace Symposium. That's really the critical event that led to our success at creating a filmmaking community because that's where I met Scott Belyea. He had grown up here and had moved to Vancouver to become a filmmaker. He was one of the artists at the Symposium and screened one of his first short films. I met him there, saw his film, and asked if we could screen it at our festival in the spring. He said sure, and then I phoned him a week or so later about teaching a workshop at the fest. He's been coming to the fest every year for all nine years and has led every major training initiative that we've done. Those early workshops focused on youth and started as two-hour workshops which became two-day workshops in 2009 and then culminated with a two-week internship project for older teens and adults in 2012, and that led to the creation of PRIMAA, the filmmakers' cooperative. Many of the filmmakers in the region had their introduction to filmmaking in one of those workshops or as an intern, actor, or crew member on The Horizon Project, the short film that Scott wrote and directed that was shot here in 2012. The whole process snowballed from there. The first festival then took place at the end of March in 2007. All in all, a short turnaround time from idea to fest: five and a half months.

How did you find films for the first year, especially since you were looking for shorts?

We only screened five packages of short films in 2007, our first year. I got the two Oscar packages from the distributor. I emailed Kerrie Long, Producer of the Edmonton International Film Festival, and told her that I was starting a film festival and could she please give me the contact info for some of the short films I saw there. So I put together two packages of films that I'd seen at the Edmonton International Film Festival. And then I put together a package of films from filmmakers who would be at the fest including my short film, two of Scott's films, three other films that had been made by current or past Peace Region residents, and a film by Julie Anne Meerschwam from New York. She also came to the fest and taught a couple of workshops. We also screened FIDO, a zombie comedy feature film, at midnight on the Friday of the fest. That worked out so well that a few years later, we started screening a Psycho Shorts package of horror shorts at midnight on Friday preceded by a Pizza Party, and that has been a big hit.

For the first couple of years, we were strictly invitational—the "best of" selections from other festivals as well as films that were connected to our region in some way. There was no submission process at all.

Then you started taking submissions, but you made the decision to not charge a submission fee. What led to that decision?

Because we didn't depend on submissions for programming the fest in the early years, we never really promoted that we were accepting submissions, so there never was a submission fee. But once we started using FilmFreeway as a submission platform for our 2015 fest, the number of submissions skyrocketed. We received 3,780 submissions, but only 37 of them were accepted as part of the 95 Official Selections that were eligible for juried awards. There were another 26 films that were part of the Oscar packages or the Frantic48 film challenge so we screened a total of 121 films. Counting the films I'd seen at other festivals or that I'd heard about, we considered 4,400 films and selected 95 of them. The percentage of our program that is getting selected from submissions is growing every year. We have stayed with a policy of not charging a submission fee because we don't want to compete with other film festivals for submissions. Filmmakers can max out their submission budget on all their top festival choices and still be able to submit to us.

I can't even fathom 3,800 unsolicited submissions! How do you review all of those—plus the additional 600 you consider?

I was fairly successful at growing our programming team quite quickly and devised a system that would coordinate everyone's efforts. We ended up with 18 people, and just plowed through them as well as we could considering how big a jump it was from our previous year when we received 625 submissions.

However, one of the results of not charging a submission fee is that we don't make any promises that a film is going to be watched from beginning to end. The beginning and the ending are watched, but a lot of the middle will be skipped if the acting or sound is poor, or if the subtitles are too difficult to read. Since such a film doesn't stand a chance of being selected, why should we spend the time to watch it in its entirety when there are so many others to watch? If you paid a submission fee, one would think that's an expectation. Still, our programming team is very clear on what our selection criteria are, and every film that meets those criteria is carefully considered.

Do you mention this in your rules and regulations—that, because there's no submission fee, films may not be watched in their entirety?

Because there's no submission fee, filmmakers often don't read the rules and regulations and we often have to disqualify films that are longer than our maximum length or their completion dates are too old to be eligible. I'm not sure it would deter anyone if they knew that. I mean, the whole point is that it's not costing them anything for their film to be considered, but you're right, I should add that point. Basically, we see filmmakers as suppliers. When a supplier wants to deal with somebody, they say here's my product. We take a look at it, and if we want to use it, we'll pay for it. We pay screening fees for every film that is programmed. I know that is not the norm for most film festivals. That is another aspect that makes us different.

For the first year's event, what was your greatest fear—other than public speaking?

It ended up a lot bigger than I thought it was going to be. I thought, originally, we would have one or two film packages, and it ended up being five film packages. Then we added workshops and a panel. My biggest fear was that it would be a huge failure. I'm a perfectionist, so obviously it was very stressful, since I was doing something that I had no idea how to do. I was completely unqualified.

And, of course, I feared public speaking. I had to force myself to do it. I've been forcing myself to do things ever since. I always laugh when people think I must enjoy it! But the end result is always extremely rewarding, and so far, that has made it all worthwhile.

How do you define success?

There are two different answers based on the two different aspects of our mission statement. First, I want at least one person in the audience to be genuinely touched—to laugh out loud, or to have insight into something they never thought of. Short films, minute for minute, are more powerful than any feature film. They have that potential.

Secondly, I want the filmmaking community to be strengthened. The underlying reason for the whole film festival was to create, to inspire, and to develop a filmmaking community. Nowadays, if you don't have filmmakers making films in your region, it's almost as if you don't exist. And now we have a filmmaking community that is creating more work every year so I'm very excited about that.

What has been your most unexpected success?

Our school program was something that I never planned and it's become a huge success. A high school class from a school 135 km (84 miles) away asked to watch a package of films while they were in town for a workshop that we offered to schools at our first fest. Then, the next year, a few more classes attended screenings as well. This year, 1,730 students attended one of five film packages specifically for schools. As a film festival that's not specifically a children's film festival, the number of students attending the fest has definitely been an unexpected success.

Tell me about how you are funded. There are obviously different corporate structures than we have here in the States. Are you a not-for-profit organization?

Since the beginning, the festival has been a production of Grande Prairie Live Theatre which is a community theatre and non-profit charitable organization. I had volunteered with them as a playwright and Assistant Director so it made sense to approach them about putting on the festival. We've always been eligible for grants, and for the first few years, most of our funding was from grants in addition to ticket sales. In the early years, funders are usually quite happy to help support you, but you've got to grow your attendance numbers fast because often those grants are just meant to help you get started. Then you need to get a lot more financially sustainable.

Grants are still important. However, now we get more cash and gift-in-kind sponsorships which together provide more funding than grants. Ticket sales are growing every year, and the City and County help with support as well. It's nice to have lots of different funding sources. It's always dangerous to depend on only a few.

How do you develop your audiences?

Word-of-mouth is the only thing that ultimately works. You have to supplement that with advertising, but if you don't have word-of-mouth working for you, the advertising won't work either. Most of the people who come to our fest have never been to one before coming to ours. Advertising rarely if ever gets people in the door for the first time, especially for short films. Someone they know has to tell them about it. But once they attend, they become fans and tell other people about it. Attendance has grown 25 percent annually as a result.

The school program is our most effective outreach program. We have five film packages for schools, one each for students in grades one to three, grades four to six, grades six to nine, grades nine to twelve Social Studies, and grades nine to twelve English/Languages. As students get older and into high school, they start coming to the fest on their own, not just as part of a school group. We had about 450 different high school students attend one or both of our high school packages and, in our intros, we tell them about the Pizza Party and Psycho Shorts Friday night. The pizza party starts at 11:15, and Psycho Shorts, the horror shorts, start at midnight. A lot of those high school kids watch the films in the school program and enjoy them much more than they think they will, so then they come to Psycho Shorts and love it, and then they start coming every year to multiple packages.

Do you have a board of directors?

The community theater has a Board of Directors which provides financial governance. We've always had artistic freedom so it has been a great relationship all these years.

Do you have any other paid staff?

The festival itself doesn't have any paid staff. Grande Prairie Live Theatre has a full-time manager, box office coordinator, and a bookkeeper. It's wonderful to have them working on the fest for the week that it's on, but GPLT also has many other productions during the year. The majority of those productions are put on by volunteers since GPLT is a community theatre.

Would you consider the job to be full-time?

It's been full-time for six years. This year I'll put in 2,800 hours. It's more than full-time actually.

Do you have an exit strategy? Do you see yourself with Reel Shorts in ten years, or do you feel that one day, you can get out?

I will have succeeded when I can step down, and it goes on without me. At some point in time, it has to be sustainable. We need to keep growing it, growing the funding sources to the point where I can step down and we can afford to replace me. Otherwise, that's not sustainable. I'm not sure if I'll be doing it ten years from now. I only commit for one year at a time.

While I enjoy the results, working fewer hours would be nice and I think that's in the foreseeable future. But at some point, if I step down and it just peters along for a year or two and then dies, so be it, but that would be my failure. Just like having a child, your ultimate success is when they're grown up and off in the world on their own.

That sounds so mature. It's not what I usually hear—especially from founders who are more controlling.

The challenge is when the festival becomes so intertwined with the founder that when the founder leaves, it can devastate the festival. It can't just depend on one person. It has to be our festival, everybody's festival. It cannot just depend on me. I think that's every founder's challenge: how to separate the festival from themselves, so they can actually get out. That is the ultimate measure of success. That will be my next challenge.

I know that you program many films you see at other festivals. How many other festivals do you attend each year?

There's only one that I always go to, the Palm Springs International ShortFest.

For the rest, I try to mix it up quite a bit. In 2014, I went to TIFF, the Austin Film Festival, and the Whistler Film Festival. This year, I went to the Calgary International Film Festival and Edmonton International Film Festival. While I found several short films at Austin last year, I went to TIFF more to attend the symposium and find potential jury members.

Since I no longer have to go to festivals to find films, thanks to receiving so many submissions, attending other fests has become more about seeing how they're run and what the audience and filmmaker experience is like rather than primarily programming from them. We will obviously never be like TIFF, and we have no desire to be like TIFF, but it was great to be there and to see what really works for them. Certainly, at the Austin Film Festival, there were interesting things to learn because they have a great conference. Every film festival has its own personality and has its own priorities. I pick up ideas and processes at every festival I attend.

Who pays for you to go to all these festivals?

That's an advantage of being a volunteer. Because I'm not paid a salary, there's money to pay my travel expenses. I include it in the budget, and I go, but I spend as little as possible while doing it. It's part of our programming expenses. But truthfully, just seeing a festival from the outside is so important, because with your own festival, you're so in the trenches on the inside that you have no perspective.

I agree. It's important to attend other events and learn from them. Most of them want to share, especially with new events.

Have you ever had a program you implemented that just didn't work out well?

We've had ones that we stopped, but not because they didn't work well. During the summer of 2012, we had a two-week internship for filmmakers. Scott Belyea brought four professionals from Vancouver, and we had a local sound guy. They brought a five-ton truck full of gear. We had two days of training on everything for the interns, six days of shooting, and then a day in the lab editing. We shot an epic post-apocalyptic short film. None of the locations had running water. No location had electricity. Three of the days were shot outside during a heat wave in a black bus with the windows closed. Every day was over 30°C (86° F). We had underage actors. We were having heat exhaustion issues. That one just about killed me from the stress. But it did what it was supposed to do. A filmmaking community formed, and from that, a filmmakers' cooperative formed, and many more short films have been made since then.

Looking back, would you have changed any of your original vision?

No, I wouldn't change anything. Meeting Scott and collaborating with him on the training initiatives was the key to what I most wanted to achieve. I can't imagine what the festival would be like if I hadn't met him. And we get a lot of feedback from people so the fest has grown organically in the right directions. We give questionnaires to everybody who'll give us their opinions (and we give them chocolate as a thank-you which really works), and that feedback has led our direction every year. The school program has grown so dramatically and much of that has been from teacher feedback. I wish I wouldn't get so stressed, but it has all worked out.

Where do you see Reel Shorts in five years?

I see it getting bigger. Our biggest challenge is venue space. There was a Landmark Cinema, but they closed last summer. The Cineplex here is really busy, and they won't give us a Friday or Saturday night. There's a college with two venues, one of which has 500 seats, but there are far more groups that want to book it than they can handle. Theater space is a community resource that's completely overbooked.

There are plans for a performing and media arts center to be built here at some point in the future. I sincerely hope that it will have three screens that we can use. That would be so fantastic.

Other than that, I'd like to grow the school program, and maybe have it tour. I expect that we'll continue to grow and that we'll be offering more year-round programming as well as industry programming during the fest.

What are you most proud of? What have you implemented that you think will have the longest impact on the festival?

Definitely the formation of a filmmaking community in the region is what I'm absolutely the most proud of, and it will have the longest impact. Local businesses can now get commercials made locally rather than bringing crews from Edmonton or Calgary, and that has an impact. I also hope we've opened students' minds with our school packages.

Hopefully, in a couple of years, we'll have a feature film shot here. The fest has created opportunities for young people too. One of our filmmakers at the 2015 fest was 19 years old, and it was her third year with a film in the fest. Her only training had been through festival initiatives. She's written, directed, and acted in her movies, and they've gone on to screen at other festivals. That would not have happened without the festival, and certainly not without Scott.

What challenges do you see for future film festivals?

The challenge is that you can watch anything online now. So what draws people in? Of course, that's the experience. When there are so many choices for entertainment, getting people's attention is a challenge, and every year it's going to be more and more of a challenge. Really, it comes down to curation, particularly with short films and how they're put together, and the filmmakers who are attending because that's an experience you can't get online.

Finally, what words of wisdom do you have for anyone who wants to create a film festival?

As with most things, it's harder than it looks. There are people who make it look easy, but many festival directors look like I do during their events—glazed eyes and sleepwalking through the day because they've been working 18-hour days.

There has to be a reason for starting the film festival that the community can support. Ultimately, the community has to adopt it, and take ownership of it. That's where your funders come from, your audience, and your volunteers. They have to want to become involved. Obviously, the founder is the one who starts it, but if nobody else grabs onto it, it won't make it past the first year or two.

ERIK JAMBOR
Sidewalk Moving Picture Festival

Erik Jambor co-founded the Sidewalk Moving Picture Festival in Birmingham, Alabama in 1999, serving as Director for its first eight years and growing the event into a filmmaker favorite and one of Time Magazine's "Film Festivals For the Rest of Us." While at Sidewalk he developed and produced year-round programming, including the organization's inaugural Birmingham Shout, the first LGBTQ film festival in Alabama. Erik ran the 2007 BendFilm Festival in Bend, Oregon, and from 2008—2014 served as Executive Director of Indie Memphis. During his seven years at the helm, Indie Memphis was included in five of *MovieMaker Magazine's* annual film festival rankings, most recently in 2014 when it was named as both one of the "25 Coolest Film Festivals in the World" and one of "50 Film Festivals Worth the Entry Fee." In 2015, Erik was presented with Indie Memphis' inaugural Vision Award and served as President of the New Filmmaker jury at the Biografilm Festival in Bologna, Italy. He has also served on juries for Slamdance, SXSW, Atlanta, Nashville, Oxford and RiverRun.

What was your background prior to starting Sidewalk?

I grew up in Birmingham, Alabama. When I was nine or ten years old, my parents gave me a Super-8 film camera. I made backyard adventure films with my friends, and stop-motion animated films with my Star Wars action figures, both with plenty of hand-scratched laser blasts. In high school, I interned at a local production house with a friend, working on commercials and industrial videos during the day, and taking over the facilities on nights and weekends to make our own films.

Florida State University was starting up their film school just as I was getting ready to go off to college, so I went down to Tallahassee to become part of their first undergraduate class. I graduated in '93 and returned to Birmingham to start up a post-production company with my high school friend. Non-linear digital editing was just beginning, so we initially focused on offline Avid work before we acquired the region's first Quantel Henry and added compositing and finishing to the mix. We mainly worked on high-end image commercials for hospitals, banks and the like, but after a few years,

I was reminded that I didn't go to film school to make TV commercials. So, I rallied the troops, pulled in some of my friends from film school, and made a short film that I hoped would play the festival circuit.

From the little I knew of film festivals, it seemed that it would be best to make a really short short that could easily be programmed in front a feature, and since in 1995 the best features seemed to be screening from 35mm prints, I wanted to shoot on 35mm and also have a couple of 35mm prints available for festival screenings. The short was called *Gamalost,* and it ended up being only 6 minutes and 40 seconds long with credits. It premiered at the Seattle International Film Festival in 1996 (where it actually was programmed in front of a 35mm feature), and went on to screen at a dozen or so festivals around the world, winning its category at the old WorldFest Charleston that year.

Was there an event that spurred your desire to start a festival?

Taking *Gamalost* out on the festival circuit provided the first bits of inspiration for me. I was knocked out of my chair by films I knew nothing about; it was an exciting, visceral experience. The festival environment seemed like the ideal way to see a movie, where you're choosing something to see because the title intrigues you, or you're captivated by the picture in the program, or maybe the synopsis raises a question that you want answered. Certainly you're walking into a screening without having been bombarded by the marketing efforts you get with studio releases. Not knowing where the filmmaker is going to take you is always a lot of fun. Bruce McDonald's *Hard Core Logo* at Slamdance is probably the example of this that had the biggest impact on me, and Slamdance itself ended up being a huge catalyst.

Back home in Birmingham, talking with friends about the festival experience and the films I was excited about, the conversation soon shifted to the idea of us starting up our own festival. There were three of us at the beginning: Wayne Franklin and Kelli McCall (who later became Kelli Franklin when they married), and me. We all worked in film and video production and wanted a way to bring films to our city, and Slamdance's "by filmmakers for filmmakers" slogan made us feel like we could do it too. We were filmmakers, so why not? Our team solidified when former MTV VJ and current SiriusXM host Alan Hunter joined the cause. He had a production company in town and was one of the leads in *Gamalost*. Alan was instrumental in getting us beyond the brainstorming phase and was our founding Board President, a position he held for the festival's first fifteen years.

When you were concocting this, were you thinking about the audience for your event, or did it evolve?

Right off the bat, our tagline was "new films for a new audience." We wanted to bring new independent films to an audience that otherwise wouldn't be able to see them, and we were as excited about building that audience as we were about bringing new films to our hometown.

At the time, there really was no other way for independent filmmakers to screen their work in the area. This was the late 1990s, way before VOD and online streaming services; Netflix was just getting started with their DVD business. The theatre chains in Birmingham were only booking the larger studio releases and the closest Art House Cinema was the Capri Theatre, 90 miles away in Montgomery. We felt like this worked to our benefit in a couple of ways. First off, Sidewalk could offer filmmakers a chance to screen their work to an unspoiled audience, so to speak. Second, we'd be able to engage that audience by offering them films they couldn't see anywhere else, and might never have an opportunity to see again. Of course, introducing the concept of "independent film" to Birmingham meant we first had to convince folks that we weren't going to just run a bunch of black and white artsy-fartsy porno flicks. (That was an actual concern that came up in those early years.)

With pretty much no existing audience for independent film in the area, we wanted our festival to be something that would appeal to local film-lovers at large. Since we'd be running films that no one in Birmingham had likely ever heard of, we wanted the event itself to be a draw. Our film festival needed to truly be a festival: it needed to be festive and fun to lure folks in for the films we wanted to show them.

Downtown Birmingham didn't have a lot going on at the time, but it did have a handful of very cool venues within a few blocks of each other and centered around the 2,300-seat Alabama Theatre, as well as several vacant storefront locations that could be turned into screening rooms. Our big idea was to model our film festival after a downtown music festival called City Stages, which was Birmingham's main music event at the time. They would close off the downtown streets, put music stages at major intersections, and fence the whole thing off. Your pass would get you in and let you wander from stage to stage to see whatever you wanted to see.

We wanted to do the same thing with Sidewalk. Our venues were initially all on the same couple of blocks, so we wanted to close off the street, fence the whole thing off, and have music stages and other street carnival fun to help attract a crowd and give them something to do between screenings. Your day or weekend pass would get you into the festival area, and if you happened to find yourself in a film that wasn't your cup of tea, you could easily wander out of the theatre and try something else.

How long was the time between the initiating spark and the first event?

It took a few years. We started talking in 1996 and were shooting to have Sidewalk's first edition take place in the Fall of 1998, but everything took longer than expected and we had to push it to May of 1999.

We were essentially making things up as we went along and it took a couple of key connections to get things on track. On the film festival side of things, when out at Slamdance trying to gather advice about starting our festival, questions seemed to all end up being directed to Gabe Wardell, Skizz Cyzyk, and Steve Montal, and their advice was crucial as we were getting everything figured out.

The actual event logistics were the big unexpected challenge, and it wasn't until event producer Keri Lane joined our team a couple of months before the festival that we realized how much we hadn't considered. She had been producing music festivals and outdoor film screenings for a number of years and knew the answers to the questions we didn't know needed to be asked about beer permits, street closures, site setup, equipment rentals, all the really essential bits, and was able to get the event production on track to hit our advertised festival dates. All those bits of logistics would normally have taken four to six months of planning; she was able to make it happen in less than two.

We still felt like Sidewalk needed to be a Fall festival, so we moved it to October for 2000, which gave us an extra five months to get our second year figured out. Of course, that put us right in the middle of the College Football season, which ended up being a pretty significant conflict. We thought we'd attract a different audience, but spent years praying that the SEC football schedule wouldn't put big Alabama or Auburn games on our festival weekend. I figured it was an unavoidable conflict, because we were trying to get away from the summer heat and humidity, but Sidewalk moved up to August a couple of years ago—ahead of the college football season—and the shift seems to have really benefited for them both in terms of audience and volunteer participation. I don't think the temperature has affected us at all

Going into the event that first year, what were your biggest fears?

We were worried that nobody one would show up. We didn't have any actual data that said the town wanted a film festival, or that there was any demand for it. We just knew we wanted it, and we figured that there were a lot of people like us. At the very least, we expected our street carnival to be the hook that would attract people who didn't know anything about independent film.

That first year, our main sponsor was Birmingham Beverage. The owner was a huge supporter and I remember running into him the Saturday of that first festival. it was the middle of the afternoon of a beautiful Spring day, and the streets were empty. The festival looked dead. Bands were playing to almost no one. He looked around at the empty streets and said, "Congrats on the festival, but where is everybody?" I led him over to our nearest venue, one of the vacant storefronts that we had turned into a screening room. When he opened the door, people literally fell onto the sidewalk. The theater was packed way past capacity, and folks had been leaning against the door.

It turned out our attendees just wanted to see the films; they weren't coming to see the live music or the poetry readings. They didn't want to miss any of the films and would just go from one film to another. By year three we had dropped the street festival part entirely and stopped closing off the streets, though I'm glad that the festival has grown enough to bring back some of those concepts in recent years.

So, the biggest fear, that no one would come, was unfounded. And everyone came for what we really wanted to focus on: the films. We didn't have to trick them into attending at all.

What was your budget for the first year?

It was a shoestring operation, held together with rubber bands and scotch tape. I don't recall what our actual budget was, but I do remember how little we knew at the start. Our scale was way off and we imagined that we'd be able to land massive sponsorships that would allow me to leave my full-time editing job and be the festival director. I did leave my job to take the festival gig, but it took years develop an actual salary.

Of course, even with a shoestring budget, we knew there were certain areas where we didn't want to cut corners. The printed program was one. It's really one of the few records of the festival that exists after the event is over, and it ends up functioning as a sales piece for the next year's event. Film festivals can be a pretty abstract concept to pitch to sponsors, and a physical book can really help them understand what the event is all about, while also giving them an impression of the festival's content, quality, and overall aesthetic. For our first year, we partnered with Birmingham Magazine to produce a nice glossy magazine format that everyone loved, but which ended up being too expensive to repeat for our second year. Ultimately, content, design and layout are way more important than pricey paper.

From the onset, you went the route of forming as a 501(c)(3) non-profit organization. Why?

It just seemed like it was what we were supposed to do. We were forming an arts organization, so we needed to be a non-profit. Much of the funding that sustained us over the years wouldn't have been possible if we didn't have 501(c)3 status: grants, donations, etc. Companies that we'd approach for cash sponsorships or other types of support were reassured that we were a non-profit, and sometimes they required it.

We applied for our non-profit status early in our planning, and received it in November of 1998. Another non-profit served as our fiscal agent in the early planning, but it helped to be able to tell folks that we had applied for our own 501(c)3 status. It was even nicer to be able to have the IRS letter of determination in hand.

Over time, did the need to be a non-profit become more or less important?

Honestly, I think it is the only way to go, unless you're doing something on the scale of SXSW, where your attendance numbers can really attract large corporate sponsors and massive ticket revenue. From a grant point of view, it is almost always required, and budgets are always so tight that it would be tough to eliminate any category of funding.

How did you find your original board members?

Our board members were originally the small team who were making it all happen. We started with five: the three co-founders, plus Alan Hunter and Michele Forman, who had recently returned to Birmingham after working with Spike Lee up in New York. By our third year we started getting serious about what kind of board we needed. By then we had proven that Birmingham wanted a film festival like the one we had created, and we could approach local business leaders about joining us, which in turn helped us increase our connections to funders and slowly increase our annual budget.

How did you decide on the initial programming strategy? How did it evolve over the years?

Initially, we were just trying to find a way to bring our favorite festival films to Birmingham. That first year included *Hard Core Logo*, Lance Mungia's *Six-String Samurai*, Heidi Van Lier's *Chi Girl*, and Adam Lamas' *Cry Havoc*; all of those, incidentally, were films we "discovered" at Slamdance. Shorts included Bruce McDonald's *Elimination Dance*, Mike Mitchell's *Herd*, which starred the beloved Kent Osborne (*Hannah Takes the Stairs*, *How to Cheat*, *Uncle Kent 2*), *More* by Kent's brother Mark (who's animated feature adaptation of *The Little Prince* is about to be released), and Don Hertzfeldt's *Billy's Balloon*.

Herd and *Billy's Balloon* we actually so popular that to satisfy demand we added spontaneous encore screenings wherever we could that first weekend. For our second festival in 2000, Kent Osborne came in with *Dropping Out*, the feature he made with his brother that premiered at Sundance that year—it's still one of my top ten film festival favorites—and he was thrilled (and a bit embarrassed) to discover that our screenings of Herd had turned him into a Sidewalk celebrity. He was recognized all over the festival; everyone knew who he was and wanted to shake his hand.

There were also a several films by filmmakers from Birmingham and other parts of Alabama that were part of that first festival and helped lay the foundation for the local filmmaking scene that would rise up over the next few years. Norton Dill's *Music in their Bones: The Music and People of Sand Mountain* was a standout that set the stage for locally produced documentaries about Alabama art and culture. Short films included *99 Threadwaxing* by Alabama native Margret Brown (who went on to make *The Order of Myths* and *The Great Invisible*) and *Webheads* by then high school students Erik Horn and Gates Bradley.

As we added venues, I started putting together threads of programming that would weave through the schedule. Essentially, it allowed us to pitch the festival as a general movie-going experience that offered something for everybody. If you wanted to see edgy new features by first-time filmmakers, you could follow a thread that would allow you to see those, or if you really just cared about the docs, you could follow that thread and pretend we were a documentary fest. Ditto for the short films and the local work. That strategy ended up being a defining aspect of the event. All the venues were (and still are) within walking distance, and you could wander from venue to venue, but would always have what seemed like a sensible path through the maze of programs.

Unavoidable conflicts actually became another signature, because aside from the rare encore screening, we only ran films once. If you missed something you later heard was great, you'd pretty much be out of luck. But that created an energy that I think made attendees have to pay more attention to what we were showing and try to plan out their schedule—at the same time the pass-structure allowed folks to be spontaneous and roll with buzz that might be building at any particular moment.

Can you talk about some of the additional programs over the years that you tried to implement?

There are two programs that worked really, really well: the Sidewalk Salon and the Sidewalk Scramble, both of which are still going strong.

The annual festival had become a catalyst for local filmmakers, and more people were making films to submit to the festival each year, but they didn't really have a way to connect in the off-season. We wanted to create a social gathering, a Sidewalk "Salon," that would feature a guest speaker and give folks a reason to get together regularly and help keep the filmmaking community connected.

One of our local hangouts, Rojo on Highland Avenue, had very cool, casual space and was willing to host the Salons one Monday a month, when they usually weren't open. Best of all, they put out free appetizers and opened up their bar. The bar really was key, because you'd have professional cinematographers, key grips and other crew folks stopping by just to grab a beer and chew the fat, and before you knew it, they'd be signing up to help with someone's upcoming indie project. It was certainly a great way to keep the filmmaking community engaged year round.

The Sidewalk Scramble is a weekend filmmaking challenge, and was our answer to events like the 48-Hour Film Project. We wanted to both inspire and challenge local filmmakers, hopefully in a way that would end up with a short that could stand on its own and have a life on the festival circuit. We ended up doing it maybe three or four times a year, and if nothing else, it helped give the community a reason to make films in the off-season and work on their filmmaking chops. Friendly rivalries would spring up, where some seemingly unbeatable filmmaking team would win Best of Show a couple of times, until some other team would emerge from nowhere and blow your socks off. It was tons of fun. Adam Wingard was one of the first participants with Team Bloodjet, who often traded top honors with Rob Rugan and team Zing! Boing! Splat!—and the little horror masterworks Adam created for the Scrambles presaged the feature work he would hit it big with a few years later. Most of them can be found on DVDs we produced for the early Scrambles. Fans of his work should seek them out, especially *Bag of Murder*.

The SideWrite short screenplay competition was another key program. We wanted to do something to help encourage writers in Alabama to write short scripts, so created a scriptwriting contest that had a Production Prize in addition to a Best Screenplay award. The idea was to have a local production company commit to producing the Production Prize winner each year, and to finish the film in time to premiere at Sidewalk the following year. Keeping the Production Prize separate from the Best Screenplay award allowed the production company to sit on the selection committee and pick the film that they wanted (and had the capacity and resources) to actually make, while still recognizing the script that might be the "best" without those considerations. A few years into the program, that model proved to be tough to keep going—there were only so many production companies who were able to commit to the concept—and SideWrite dropped the Production Prize, while expanding to accept short screenplays from outside of Alabama.

We also started Alabama's first gay and lesbian film festival in 2006, Birmingham Shout. It was originally a stand-alone festival, which took place in the Spring to help fill our year-round calendar. Malcolm Ingram's *Small Town Gay Bar* opened our inaugural year, and Malcolm's enthusiasm for what we were trying to do really helped put that event on the map. A few years ago, it was merged into Sidewalk's weekend in the Fall, and the energies of the two festivals feed off each other nicely. I'm really happy it has grown as much as it has.

Looking back, what aspects of the festival would you have implemented differently?

Closing off the streets and trying to keep our festival footprint small enough to allow us fence it all off was a bad idea. We could have skipped over a lot of expensive headaches if we had realized how unnecessary it was. We got smart by our third year, did away with the street closures and fencing, and were able to add a fantastic venue just two blocks away, the 500-seat Carver Theatre at the Alabama Jazz Hall of Fame. It was still important to have of a solid density of activity around the Alabama Theatre, which served as the heart of the festival, and we did our best to keep all of our venues nearby, or at least an easy walk away.

What contribution are you most proud of, that believe has the biggest impact on the event?

The environment and overall vibe of the festival was really key to Sidewalk's early success. It was created as a fun, casual event that would attract an audience that had never been to a film festival before. A friend once described the festival's appeal as being its "intimate accessibility," which I think is right on the money. We want our attendees to feel as much a part of the excitement as the filmmakers coming in to present their work. The festival was imagined without velvet ropes and VIP lounges, so filmmakers would just hang out with general attendees. Everyone would mix and mingle.

We also wanted to make sure that the filmmakers really got to know each other, and created a "filmmaker retreat" before the Opening Night events kicked off. It functioned as a field trip with a meet-and-greet lunch. Those who were already friends also had plenty of opportunities to catch up with each other, so that once the Opening Night fun began, it was easier for them to meet and hang with the festival audience.

The connections that were created were always a priority; it was exciting to see what collaborations might develop from one year to a next. We premiered Andrew Bujalski's *Funny Ha Ha* in 2002. It played the Woodstock Film Festival the same weekend, but Andrew and Kate Dollenmayer came to Sidewalk and sent their producer to Woodstock, because they heard good things about our fest and a number of filmmakers Andrew met at Sidewalk ended up working on his second feature, Mutual Appreciation.

You left Sidewalk in 2006. What was next for you?

After Sidewalk, I ran the fourth edition of the BendFilm Festival in Bend, Oregon, and then served as Executive Director of Indie Memphis from 2007 through 2014. Indie Memphis was an unexpected opportunity to do more with the ideas we were working with at Sidewalk: building community and connecting filmmakers and attendees with that "intimate accessibility" concept.

We grew our attendance from under 4,000 to a high of 12,000, and expanded from one venue to four, all within a couple of blocks of each other in a theatre district that was being redeveloped. With locally-owned restaurants, bars and shops connecting the venues, the festival developed a unique neighborhood vibe that appealed to both local attendees and to the filmmakers and special guests coming in from around the country. During those seven years, Indie Memphis was frequently in *MovieMaker Magazine's* annual rankings. It was named one of their "Coolest Film Festivals" in 2009 and 2014, and made their "Worth the Entry Fee" list in 2011, 2013, and 2014.

You left Indie Memphis in 2015, after an amazing run. What are you doing now?

I am focusing on festival programming and consulting now, and am working on a set of online tools and resources for local and regional film festivals: templates and forms and guidelines that I've developed of the past seventeen years. Stay tuned for details!

What are the challenges you see for the future of festivals?

For so long the big challenge was just trying to get people to understand what "independent films" were. Now it is a category on Netflix and Apple TV, and on-demand from your cable provider. You don't have to live in a city with an Art House theatre, you can just sit on your couch and watch the latest indie releases.

Of course, it is much easier to just stay home and watch films in your living room, so festivals have to offer an experience that warrants the hassle of leaving the house and finding a place to park. Obviously, seeing a film in a theatre with an audience, especially a film festival audience, is a whole different experience than your living room can offer, but for film festivals to survive, it is pretty much essential to give attendees an opportunity to interact with filmmakers and guests through post-screening Q&A sessions, talkbacks, meet-and-greets, etc. It's all about building connections and community.

Final question: What words of wisdom would you give to someone who wants to start a new festival?

Volunteers are the key to a successful event. You need to develop a team of volunteers—a real community—that can come together and support the event, and each other, from year to year. Thank them often, reward them well, and find ways to keep them engaged and connected year-round.

Also ask yourself why you want to start a film festival in the first place. Who is it for? Why will they want to attend? And make sure someone else in your city isn't already doing the same thing.

It's very easy in major markets like New York or Los Angles to think "There are enough film festivals, we don't need any more." But not all festivals are about discovering new talent or showing premieres, a lot of them are there for the community where they take place, "bringing new films to a new audience." That's a large part of what regional festivals like Sidewalk, BendFilm, and Indie Memphis are really about. Bringing elements together to better your community. If you live in a town that is not being served the way you think it should, or would like it to be then there's a great opportunity to do something meaningful and magnificent.

JESSICA HARDIN
Pasadena International Film Festival

Jessica Hardin founded the Pasadena International Film Festival in 2013 and serves as its Executive Director. She has worked as an actor, model, dancer, singer, casting director, and teacher. Hardin is a member of SAG-AFTRA, AEA, the Smith College Club of Los Angeles, the Smith College Club of Pasadena, the Ivy League Association of Southern California, and recently created the Five Sisters Club of Pasadena.

What was your background before you started the Pasadena International Film Festival?

I'm from all over—Illinois, South Carolina, Smith College in Massachusetts. I studied at the National Theater Institute (Waterford, CT) and British American Drama Academy, (London, England) then moved to New York City, where I studied with Bill Esper.

I wanted to learn as much as I could about the industry, so I worked for a casting director and for two different talent agencies, one commercial and one theatrical. My brother moved to Los Angeles to attend graduate school at U.S.C., and when I went to visit him, I just fell in love with the city.

I was at that point in my life where I loved New York City, but it was crowded. I really wanted a little bit more space. I was missing "normal people" things… small town, suburban lifestyles, homes and gardens, cars. Los Angeles really is seductive. It's got perfect weather. So, I moved out here, and I did a little bit of acting. I also worked for a personal manager, a literary manager, and a literary agent. I did a little bit teaching too, and I still do—Shakespeare, primarily. After I married Marco, I moved to Pasadena, and that's how I was introduced to the town.

How did you come to start the film festival?

Facebook happened, and Twitter. Being in Los Angeles, it seemed like every day, I was getting emails to "fund my film," "fund my film." I said to Marco, "Everyone we know is making a movie." He was cast in an independent film that toured the festival circuit. We attended the Almeria Film Festival in Spain and the then-called Beverly Hills Film, TV and New Media Festival, here in LA. That sort of planted the seed.

Pasadena is different, because it is Los Angeles, but it is also its own city, and it's very much about festivals. They have dance, arts, music, and an Earth Festival. The only festival they didn't seem to have was a film festival. One thing led to another, and I started taking meetings. I called a couple of directors who had run film festivals here that had either folded or moved to different towns. I met with the Mayor. And through all of these meetings, I got the feedback that it would be extraordinarily difficult. But I still wanted to do it. It seemed difficult, but not impossible. It's not like we needed to have a million dollars, and I was going to buy a huge building. So, I thought, "What the hell? I'm going to go for it." It snowballed: one thing led to another, to the point that it was too late back out. Now we're here.

There were other film festivals that had been in Pasadena and disbanded?

I interviewed a lot of people and did a lot of research. There's never been a "Pasadena Film Festival," but there were a couple of festivals that had existed in the City of Pasadena. One disbanded, and The Action on Film Festival moved to Monrovia, just one town over.

When planning the first event, I wanted to make sure I wasn't infringing on anyone's turf. We joined up with a great graphic designer who designed our rose logo (Pasadena is obviously known for the Rose Bowl, and the Rose Parade).

Talk about the mission of the festival.

We wanted to do something that was a little bit different, and selfishly, I wanted to create a community. I feel like Los Angeles is tough place to meet people. Unless you grew up here, you don't have the luxury of school to create your community. I wanted to create a sense of community in Pasadena, both for residents and for filmmakers.

I also wanted to create something that didn't feel "dog eat dog." I wanted our festival to feel like "film camp," with a sense of camaraderie and good feelings: friendliness, warmth, and happiness.

And I definitely want to stay in the black. I think a lot of festivals start out thinking, "This seems like a great way to make some money." I was a bit more realistic with that. I'd rather do it for a few years and not make tons of money, but do it right. I wanted to create an event from the filmmaker's perspective. Marco, my husband and creative director, felt that when he went to other festivals, especially the L.A. Film Festival, that it was no longer about independent films as much as it's about studios and stars. When Robert Redford started Sundance, it just evolved so much that it's not really what it was what it set out to do. We wanted to fill that void, and fill that niche.

How long did it take you to plan the first year?

It took two years actually, because we wanted to do it right. I'd say the toughest, toughest challenge was raising funds, especially when people don't know you. I was realistic, and I started out with really low levels of sponsorship, and just grew it from there. Of course, most sponsors want to wait until the very last minute to give you the cash, so we took a really long time. It took two years to plan. I read everything I could get my hands on, because there was a lot to learn, and I wanted to learn every facet of it.

There are so many different aspects: development, fundraising, marketing, programming. I wanted to make sure we did it right. The Film Festival Organizers group on Facebook helped a great deal. I found the group through Melanie Lynn Addington of the Oxford Film Festival. You can only read so much, and nowadays, things happen so fast that you really have to stay on top of it, and in real time. Speaking with other festival directors was a huge asset.

Some festivals have very long gestation periods, and I admire that. Others are literally thrown together in months. DC Shorts was literally thrown together in four months. SXSW was created in five or six. That is definitely not the norm. I think many people want to get into this industry, and think they can whip together an event in a few months—that is not realistic. Especially if you're coming from a place where you've never really done this.

Yes, and it would depend on if I were a trust-fund baby. If I had millions of dollars, sure, it's always easier to buy knowledge by hiring in the best people. But even then, there's still only so much you can learn in that short allotted amount of time.

I will admit that the whole process was a bit scary, because I had no idea what I didn't know. There was still that element of surprise, but I felt better having researched all that I could so I was not too blind. I figured you only get one shot. If we screwed up the first year, I would have to move to Mexico or something.

Going into that first festival, what was your greatest fear?

That no one would show up.

Which is everyone's fear, by the way.

I would imagine. I know people, myself included, who get nervous throwing a dinner party, let alone something on this scale. Of course, you're going to get nervous doing something that's never been done before, at least in your particular town, or with the particular way that you run it. You just have no idea who's going to show.

It's interesting. I've learned big cities and small towns have negatives and positives on both sides. In Los Angeles there's just so much going on. There are five red carpet events nearly every night of the week. Plus, don't think people here go out as much as they do in New York City. People are sick of driving, so it can be a challenge to get people to come out. We just gave it everything we've got, and we were fortunate in that people did show up.

What was your biggest surprise that first year?

Oh my gosh, I was really surprised that it was a lot of fun, that I enjoyed the whole experience. I was really surprised at how wonderful everyone ended up. With much of planning the festival, you're isolated on your computer. Or you work in an office with a few people. It was really nice to meet so many filmmakers, and meet so many people. Martin Sheen showed up on our first night. He just showed up in jeans and a t-shirt on Wednesday night. He was just so wonderful, and we were just thrilled to have him. There was a real sense of excitement. I was surprised at that.

Tell be about that first event: how many films did you show? How many theaters? How many days? Audience?

Our first year, we showed 86 films. We were just in one theater. There's only one theater we can rent out here that will rent out on weekends, the Laemmle. The owner, Greg Laemmle, is the descendent of Carl Laemmle, who founded Universal Pictures, and he owns a chain of independent movie theaters around the Los Angeles area. To me, if I were a filmmaker, this is where I'd want to screen my film. Anyway, we screened from Wednesday through Sunday.

That's a lot of films in one theater and five days.

It is. I thought the more films, the larger the crowds, and I think that was right. We have a lot of shorts, but we also wanted to really maintain a level of quality. I didn't want to just have films for the sake of films. We were very fortunate, I think, because we had no idea what to expect.

In the first year, we took submissions using Withoutabox. We were lucky we received about 300 submissions, and they were really, really good. I've been to some film festivals where you watch films and think, "What did they reject?"

For your first year's event, what was the budget?

We try to keep that on the down low, because it's a miracle that we even made it. I would say around $50,000.

For some festivals, that's a lot of money. Are you a 501(c)(3) non-profit?

No, we're not. We're actually a small business. I've been trying to decide whether to become a non-profit or not.

It's something that we're really back and forth with. Honestly, it hasn't been a problem with sponsors. If Wells Fargo called and said, we'll give you $50K if you become nonprofit, we would become nonprofit. Even so, most business are giving to us a marketing and advertising expense, not a charitable contribution.

I also got scared: I was told the story of a woman who started a festival, and then the board fired her. That scared the bejeezus out of me! We have this great advisory board, but one of the members had been a little unprofessional. I see how this could be an issue in the future, which is why I'm happy with an advisory board, and not a board of directors.

I'm with you on starting it as a for-profit. There are a lot of festivals that feel they have to start as non-profit, or move to non-profit because they feel that with grants, there's this pot of free money from governments. I believe there is a greater amount of money corporations are going to give it you out of their corporate funds, not their philanthropic money funds.

It's also a lot easier. Don't forget you have to pay someone to write those grants. I did a cost-benefit analysis. I could go for a $5,000 grant, but I would have to pay someone $5,000 to write it. That's been a reservation of mine. Either I have to learn how to write grants, or hire someone to do it. Then it's always a crapshoot. Will we get the money, will we not?

We're a small business, and whether you're a small business or a non-profit it doesn't seem like there's the opportunity to make huge amounts of money, especially as a film festival.

Talk about your programming strategy. How did you determine what types of films you were going to program that first year? Has that changed for the second year?

When I first started, everyone asked, "what's your niche? What's your genre?" I know there are festivals for everyone—even a festival for gay surfers. They get really, really specific. I wanted to leave our programming as open as possible, so we could review as many films as possible, and pick the very best from what we've received. I only had one screener: Marco. He and I watched everything.

I learned that programming international films, especially features, is tough. We had a Korean feature that we loved. The filmmaker wasn't able to come out, because the flights are insanely expensive, and we had no budget to pay for his travel. My dad sent letters to hundreds of Korean churches and restaurants to drum up business for the film. Unfortunately, it didn't help.

As for programming shorts, we like to include as many as possible. It's just common sense: you've got a theater for two hours, you can show one feature, or you show ten shorts. You're going to have a much bigger audience with the ten films.

Do you program groups of films by theme or genre?

Yeah, that's the most creative part, designing our blocks. Instead of calling blocks "Showcase 1," we try to come up with creative titles: the horror block is "Something Wicked This Way Comes." One year, we had a "Steam Punk" block and a "Power Girl" block. They come about based on what is available to us. Last year I saw a heavy amount of films dealing with Alzheimer's, dementia, the elderly, or taking care of your aging parent films, which makes sense in the aftermath of *Still Alice* with Julianne Moore.

We've tried to hit the major segments. We try to have something for kids. This year we have a girls' school that's interested in coming, so we programmed a couple of blocks that were really great for teenagers. That alone is a challenge, because we don't want anything too adult, though we don't want cartoons for children, either.

I think programming for kids is difficult. I think the tendency is to go really babyish, when in truth, if you show them sophisticated films, they get it.

Right. We had a really cute film called *"Lilly Tells."* It's about a six-year-old girl who's giving her reviews of major movies. She says words like "ass" and "damn." We warned parents first. I worked with kids before and hoped that parents wouldn't get up in arms, and they didn't. It's such an adorable movie.

Do you curate films?

The first year, I was excited because Katie Couric and Jada Pinkett Smith were marketing the film *Not My Life,* about human trafficking, with Glenn Close narrating. This was one of the few films I reached out to. They sent their movie, and even paid the submission fee.

But I found that curated films don't really garner a lot of attention—or a lot of audience members. We try to stick with submitted films, because I know that if they've submitted, the filmmakers have a vested interest in attending and bringing friends, and will have a lot of enthusiasm for your festival.

Can I get off topic?

Sure.

As I researched festivals, I was surprised that there are a lot of festivals with some shady business practices.

I would agree.

You must know on some level that there are a lot of film festivals that do this to try to make a quick buck. That's what I try to warn filmmakers, especially in Los Angeles. Be leery when you see super pricey submission fees.

The first festival we went to was the Beverly Hills Film TV, and New Media Festival. It wasn't even in Beverly Hills. I don't know how they got to call it that. I'm sure they knew the name would garner interest.

There are festivals that charge for an award. We were offering an award to Eric Roberts. His wife asked if there was a charge. She mentioned he'd been offered awards, but would be charged. I thought, "Oh my Lord!"

Yes, I've heard of that: festivals that charge for trophies, exorbitant entry fees with bogus screenings. A few years ago, there was a festival in the UK that was poorly run, that asked filmmakers to stand in the streets to "sell" their films, and at the awards show, put the filmmakers in a separate room in the basement to watch via TV. Needless to say, one of the documentarians took out their camera and exposed them. I don't think that event has recovered.

I just don't get it. That's one of the reasons it took us two years to plan. We wanted to do everything well.

Building on that, how do you develop relationships with your audiences?

That's a good question. I think most of our audience is comprised of the friends of the filmmakers. They bring in a majority of people. But we're really lucky that there are a lot of publications in Pasadena. The press has been great: they do stories on us and try to get us coverage. I think it's harder in a large town.

I also understand that if somebody sees a movie once a week they're going to see a big film, like The Avengers. They're not going to see an independent film. We try to hit that group, but we know that for the most part, our audience are artists, filmmakers, actors, and writers. Which is absolutely fine with me. We've been really fortunate to have had a very happy supportive group.

How do you develop your relationship with sponsors?

I started out with a lot of research. I created a Google document of around 1,000 potential sponsors. I looked to see who else sponsored other film festivals and who has the largest advertising budgets. I think it's common sense. A lot of it's hit and miss. For every yes, there are 200 no's. We just keep trying.

I also try to make it as personable as possible. I try to attend every event in the city. Because of this, the Pasadena Film Office sponsors us, and Pasadena Water and Power. I try to develop personal relationships, and get to know people as people. That is our mission: it's all community.

I definitely wanted to under promise and over deliver. It's tougher as we get closer to the festival.

Is running the Pasadena International Film Festival a full-time job?

The first year definitely was, then things got a little bit easier. I think the hardest part was just launching it. I realized that if the sponsors and venues and filmmakers were happy—and they were—then we could relax a bit. And use that momentum to make future work a little easier and less time consuming.

I'd say definitely three months before the festival, it's totally full-time. The winter's really intense. In the summer I'm in my development phase, and it's quieter.

Do you have other staff members?

Pretty much, it's me. Marco works full-time, but helps out as well. The second year, we had five screeners. This year, I think we'll have about ten, so we're doubling it.

We have a great graphic designer, an attorney, and an accountant. We even do our own website and everything. We started out with a web designer, and he wanted so much money and he never delivered on time. But, pretty much everything from bookkeeping to adding a sponsor logo on the website at 3:00 in the morning is done by me.

How many volunteers help out during the festival?

We had about twenty. In a perfect world, they would work four hour shifts with a twelve-hour commitment. That is a big obstacle for many. We got really lucky, and have about five people who are there for the entire thing. I know it is exhausting, but it's also a lot of fun. I prefer this commitment because you really get to know people well, they get to know the festival well, and it feels like a big fun family.

What are some of the biggest challenges your festival is facing?

I would assume it's what challenges most festivals: making sure that people show up. Another challenge is that everybody wants something different and you can't make everybody happy. I think you have to make a decision: be firm, be strong about it and say, "This is what we're going to do." That can be difficult, but it helps us guide the festival to where we want to take it.

How do you define success?

Honestly, staying in the black. I talk to a lot of festivals, and not all have done so. Some have gone into their own personal savings. If we manage to get creative and crafty, and keep our expenses below our revenues, I think that's good.

Spinning off that, making filmmakers happy. As we grow, I definitely want to see filmmakers get distribution deals. They should get more press —not just to the Pasadena papers, but from the L.A. Times and the Hollywood Reporter, and Variety.

You have a great cautionary tale.

I knew you were going to bring this up. By the way, thank you and the other festival directors for their support. It was a grueling ordeal and your support is what made the whole thing bearable!

I think you took one for the team. You learned a hard lesson that now many other festivals can benefit from. Can you talk about your legal issues?

My foremost advice would be to find an excellent attorney who can help you out pro bono. We asked nearly a dozen attorneys, some of whom were compensated, to do something as simple as go over our website, to help us design legal language that would help protect us. Not one attorney felt comfortable doing that. There are so many different types of law, so many different specialties, it was absolutely ridiculous how many attorneys one person needs, and how much money that requires.

I read litigation stories now where, in my opinion, it's legalized bullying. Often times insurance companies will pay off the person threatening to sue, because that is cheaper than paying attorney's fees. It's rewarding bad behavior. It doesn't make sense to me that alleged criminals are afforded pro bono counsel, but victims of lawsuits outside of criminal law must somehow raise thousands of dollars, or must cater to the whims and desires of anyone with a pro bono attorney.

People are just gripped by fear, that's what I've witnessed, especially here in LA. It's gotten to the point where I feel the need to phone an attorney at nearly every turn. It was mind blowing to me how much power someone has just because they are an attorney: they can force you to show up, or you risk going to jail, they have access to your accounts, your bank information, your emails. It really makes me want to become an attorney, in all honesty. Lawsuit abuse is rampant. Why is there no judge assigned to sift through the millions of lawsuits (in California alone) to see which have merit and which do not, before forcing people to spend thousands (as individuals, millions altogether) on legal costs?

I think our attorneys and others thought that I was crazy or stupid, taking risks such as talking to the press, and they thought that I should keep my mouth shut. But it seemed very wrong to me that I should not tell the truth because we are scared of a couple of people simply because they are willing to work hard for no pay.

I think people just want to believe that a lawsuit is not going to happen. Just plan and prepare yourself for the worst. You don't know that.
Unfortunately, we cannot speak to this. There are articles online if you're interested. Suffice it to say, in the end, we won and it never went to trial.

It is a sad tale—and even sadder that it is true. I would concur that over the past few years, filmmakers have begin to feel more and more entitled to participate in a festival. I know of a few other festivals that have been sued for a removing a film, moving a film's time slot—even a crazy suit against Cannes for not accepting a film to begin with!

I think festivals are a business—whether it's for-profit or non-profit—it's still a business. They have to protect themselves. All of a sudden we need to worry about about something we never had to think of before, or wanted to think of before.

All anyone has to do is threaten to sue, and everyone suddenly bends over. And insurance companies just pay people off instead of really pursuing the case. For example, I was reading about Back To The Future. Did you know about Crispin Glover, the actor who played the father?

No, what happened?

> Crispin played George McFly. For the second *Back To The Future*, he wanted $1,000,000. The director said, we can't do that; come up with a realistic offer, or we're going to assume that you can't be in the movie. So he refused to be in the movie. The filmmaker used clips from the first movie—his likeness—and Crispin sued.
>
> Of course, everyone's thinking, that's stupid because you're never going to work again. You know what? The insurance company paid him $800,000 to not have to go to court. What the hell would court cost? That's why only three percent of lawsuits even go to court, because they settle.

You've learned a horrible life lesson.

> At least I learned it early! And in doing so, everyone else has learned from my experience. As business people, we need to make sure we are covered for all kinds of things: angry filmmakers, filmmakers without proper licenses or clearances, filmmakers who cause injury to others while at your event. It's smart to be prepared.

So, how have you changed your business practices?

> We have screening contracts. We updated our submission rules and agreement. I have received feedback from people saying that no other festival does this. I say, "If you don't want to sign it, that's cool. We're not screening your movie." Maybe it scares them, but I think it's smart. And like our lawyers said, if you plan to start a business, prepare to be sued. I would say that it's a lot less likely with non-profits, but if we were a non-profit, they could still come after us individually. Or worse, they would've gone after every member of the board.

Where do you see your festival in five years?

> Let's start with three. I see us growing, but I also want to maintain the boutique feeling that we have created. I like feeling warm. I like the feeling of friendliness. I like paying attention to details.

What do you think are the challenges facing film festivals in general?

> Every year we have a "Future of Entertainment" panel. It's always really interesting. To me, the Internet is a bit overwhelming. Like me, you grew up

with one newspaper, maybe a few dozen TV or cable channels.. But now, with the Internet, everyone has a YouTube channel. I think that's what I really like about film festivals: it's a three-dimensional, person-to-person experience. It is something I really miss, and I wonder if the millennial generation does. I see a great value in that, so I hope that continues.

What are you most proud of? What values do you think you've installed into the event that would be your lasting mark?

I would say I really love our "Great Gatsby" Gala. It has improved a great deal from the first year. It's a really magical night. We have stars and press come out. I wanted it to feel like a fancy wedding.

I didn't want the festival to feel like a cast of thousands. I wanted people to feel special, and events to feel intimate. I think that we achieved that. If we can keep that going, that would be great. And I really like helping other festivals as well, trying to maintain that attitude of inclusiveness, rather than exclusivity, and rather than the competing.

That's wonderful. My final question: what words of wisdom do you have for anyone who wants to start a film festival?

Get a good lawyer. Get a really good lawyer who knows a lot, who you can trust, and hopefully is also an entertainment attorney. And trust yourself. Listen to yourself. At the end of the day, no one's going to care about your festival the way you do.

JOSH LEAKE
Portland International Film Festival

Josh Leake is a film director and producer, and the founder and executive director of the Portland Film Festival, named one of the world's "coolest" film festivals by *MovieMaker Magazine*. His first film, *Emptys*, a documentary about people who collect beverage containers as their principal source of income, won first place at Tropfest New York 2012. He also produced *Glena*, a feature length documentary that premiered at Slamdance in 2014.

What inspired you to start the Portland Film Festival? What was your background?

Growing up, my grandmother would take me to see a movie every Saturday. Then in college, I majored in graphic design and German, but I took some film courses and played around with film equipment. After college, I worked as a Creative Director and ran Wells Fargo's Internet marketing campaigns. Then, after I left that job, I started my own mortgage company, which I still run today.

Back in 2009, I was dating a girl who didn't like to go to see movies, so I started the Portland Film Club so I'd have some company on my movie night outings. We are now the largest film-watching club in Oregon with approximately 2,400 members who watch a movie together each week.

Around that time, a client of mine, who knew I loved movies, suggested I make one myself. He told me about a contest where you could win $10,000 and 16 computers. So I did a one-minute video and ended up winning. With that money, I bought some film equipment. Within a couple of months, I ended up doing another contest and I won another $10,000. I started taking filmmaking classes. Then I did a short film and won Tropfest, the largest short film contest, and best of all, Hugh Jackman handed me a check for $20,000. That short film also got into a whole slew of other film festivals.

Through that experience, I got a really great education on film festivals. I thought a general interest film festival would do great in Portland. At that time in Portland, we had an international festival, but they pretty much only screened international films.

After my travels, I came back and talked to about a hundred different friends. Five of us decided to start a festival. The idea was to make it more of a filmmakers' festival with an emphasis on education. We had acting classes, screenwriting classes, pretty much everything I saw and liked at other festivals. So, I wouldn't say that we are necessarily innovators. Recreating the wheel sometimes isn't worth the effort if it's already been created.

Why do you think you are the person who created this?

Maybe it's because I was an only child, and if I wanted to do something, I had to go ahead and do it on my own. I couldn't wait around for someone else to do it.

I also know that I can't do it alone. The festival tries to bring as many partners to the table as we possibly can. This year we are getting some money from the governor's office. That's a good sign. Other festivals in our city get $500,000 from the state and it's amazing. Maybe someday, we will be there. We do a lot with very little.

What were some of your founding principles?

I was inspired by Raindance, Slamdance and Tropfest. They are really pioneers for independent thinking, independent filmmaking. The funny thing is that in our first year, a lot of films that we curated were from Raindance. A lot of them were North American premieres because Raindance has this amazing cache of European Independent film.

Did you have a community or audience in mind when you were forming the festival?

What makes us different is that I really make the festival for filmmakers. I make the festival for someone like myself who is interested in learning about films, networking with other filmmakers and meeting national press. Those are the people that I want to hang out with because we are all in it together.

A lot of times, people are afraid to share and work in a community because they think that people will steal their ideas or something. It's actually the opposite. The better the community you have, the bigger things you can do.

How long did it take for you to plan the first festival?

One of the co-founders, Jay Cornelius, was a professor I had taken classes with. He was the biggest inspiration. He had worked on other film festivals, so he became the Director of Programming. I organized venues, got sponsors, did all of the marketing, invited the speakers, the guests, the films, a lot of the curated films. Jay handled most of the submissions. Most of the entries come from submissions, so Jay had a lot of work. We have another partner, Honi Ledford. We had five or six people devote their life from April until our festival in August. It was almost like full-time jobs and none of us are paid. Jay and I put a significant amount of money behind it. Even Honi donated. She used to be a flight attendant, so she gave some of her passes for the filmmakers to come. It was a pretty amazing experience having all these people come together and put it on. A lot of comments we got were, "This feels like a five-year old festival" and to me that was so amazing.

How long was your first event? How many days?

It was seven days.

You pulled off a seven-day event with only four or five months of planning?

I went down to Tropfest in Sydney, Australia. Before that, I had mentioned to Jay that we should probably start a film festival. After I came back from Australia, he was all for it. An Australian guy owned the domain name "portlandfilmfestival.com." He wanted to sell it to me for $1,500 and it took me four weeks to buy it from him, but I got it down to $600. As soon as I had the domain name, Jay and I put up a website, set up Withoutabox, and started getting submissions. We had very little public relations, very little advertising. We just started and had no pre-festival marketing. Eventually, we did spend a lot of money on advertising. We learned a lot of things about advertising though: where to do it, where not to do it.

At one of our most successful events, we had 23,000 people log on and watch our screenwriting competition. We had local actors from Portland who read the first ten pages from four script finalists. We were so amazed that so many people would want to watch or at least at some point tune into our scriptwriting competition.

This last year, we had some films that were online and some 500,000 views of those films happened during the week of our festival.

That first year, what was your greatest fear?

That no one would show up.

Which, by the way, is everyone's fear.

And I worried that filmmakers wouldn't have fun. I own a mortgage company, and I also run a networking group for the mortgage real estate industry in Portland. The last Friday of every month, I throw a party and invite all the realtors. So I've thrown events before, and I've had 500 people showed up for one of my parties before. I've worked with bands. I've done a lot of event planning in my life, so that really helped because I was able to not necessarily worry about that madness. If you have a plan and surround yourself with people who are good at what they do, even if stuff goes wrong, the overall event will still be good.

That first year, we spent more money than we probably should have, but we just wanted to make sure that people had fun. I had a large house that was empty during our film festival the first year, so we used it to house filmmakers. The house had eight bedrooms, so it was huge. We had 32 filmmakers who stayed in that house, and they had the time of their lives. Unfortunately, that house was not available in year two. We definitely have other accommodations, but it was a really fun experience. I wish we could duplicate it, but unfortunately, getting a large house like that is hard.

Oh, I know. In the first year, I had fifteen people sleeping on my floor because that was all we could afford. Is the festival run as a for-profit or non-profit organization?

We've been non-profit since the beginning. There are other festivals in Portland that are for-profit, but for me, to be able to get government grant money and people's engagement, they can't think that I'm sitting at the back making money and using it to do whatever I want. Having a mission to support filmmakers and audiences in Portland is something that people can get behind. Whereas if you are for-profit, it's a little harder to do in our market. In other markets, it would make sense, but for us, I really felt having a non-profit would be better financially. Ultimately, I would love our festival to be self-sustaining and to do that you have to have people donate to your festival. It is great to be able to give those individual donors the ability to write that off on their taxes.

How did you select your original board?

It was our attorney, Jay, and myself.

Do you still only have these three people as a board?

Now we've got five or six. We have more women now than men. We have an accountant, some theater owners, and theater managers. We try to bring in people from our community to be on the board.

How do you choose them? Is it strategic?

The people we tend to choose are people who are involved with the festival and involved in the community. We have forty to fifty people on our advisory board, which is not our non-profit board. Our advisory board is more or less people who work in the industry, that support our event and help us when we need help. Having a larger advisory board versus an actual procedural board is sometimes better, because if you get twenty or thirty people on your board, it's a lot harder to make decisions and get things done.

How do you develop your relationship with filmmakers?

I go to other film festivals.

And how many film festivals a year do you attend?

One a month, if not more.

Are you programming films you see at other events? What percentage of films do you bring in versus submissions?

We don't curate a lot. We curate between ten and fifteen percent. There is another film festival in our town that screened 140 films this last year, and they only played five films from submissions. So that's a big difference. For me, I love independent films, and we got so many great films that other festivals have turned down. I love finding those types of films. Sure, we'll play some films from Sundance, from Raindance, but it's always awesome to find new things in submissions. Slamdance is one of my favorite film festivals ever. Slamdance is such an well curated festival.. We always play several Slamdance films because it's got that independent feel.

Talk about your programming strategy. What are you looking for? How do you evaluate? Is there anyone who helped you with it?

Our first year, I had just broken up with my girlfriend, so I totally loved all the relationship films. We programmed so many relationship films about people breaking up, people getting together. One of our VIP pass members came up to me and asked, "Did someone on programming just get dumped or something?"

We love pretty much every genre. I don't think there's a genre we wouldn't play at Portland. We try to find films that will relate to our audience. We tend to have a younger audience. Our attendees tend to be between 23 and 40 years of age. We have some older audience members, but most of the people who go to our film festival are younger and they want more social events. We tend to program music around our films. We program networking before or after our films. More women attend our festival than men, so we tend to be more cognizant of that. Our first opening night film was from a female director. We try to support and play as many good films as we can from a diverse pool of directors. We try to find unique films that tell a good story.

Have you tried a program that just doesn't seem to work?

At Sundance and at Toronto, they have late night screenings. In our first and second years, we experimented with that, but we had a very low attendance because people don't want to come out at 12:15 at night. We are moving our midnight screenings to around 10:00 pm, so that it will end around midnight. You really have to program your films around times that people will watch. Programming a film at 7:00 AM on a Saturday or a Sunday probably wouldn't work.

Right. Although depending on your audience, it might. I've been in festivals where they had packed houses at 8:00 in the morning on a Sunday. You would think no one could do that, but there is an audience for that. It also depends if ticket sales are doing well, and that's the only time when someone can see a popular film.

Let's talk stats. This last festival, how many films did you show?

We showed 145 that were officially in our program but we ended up screening more. What we typically do is leave some empty slots of theater space open so that we can end up doing a special screening or an unmarked, unnamed film. Sometimes filmmakers want to premiere their films somewhere else, and they want us to play it, but they don't want us to advertise it, so that they can get into Sundance or other venues. We are open to that. We screened another forty films, which included shorts and features. So last year, we screened some 180 films although we only advertised 145.

Some of those films came from the Beijing Independent Film Festival, which was shut down by the government. In support of them, we screened the films that were banned, but we didn't advertise it because I may want to work in China as a producer or director. We didn't put them in our program, but we screened them and we did let everyone know.

Get to the numbers: How many days was the festival? The number of venues? Audience size?

> Last year, the festival was seven days. We had between eight and twelve venues if you count some of our classrooms. And our total audience was close to 23,000.

Wow, and how many volunteers?

> 347 or something like that.

Are you a full-time paid staff member, or you are still volunteering?

> I'm a volunteer.

Do you have any full-time paid staff?

> This year is actually our first year that we've had paid staff. We had people who had contracts last year. Last year, we had maybe three people that made money from the festival. I wasn't one of them. This year, we have probably four or five people plus we are going to be paying our theater managers. But we've been primarily a volunteer everything festival.

So what is your approximate budget?

> Last year it was around $80,00 to $100,000.

You pull off such a large event for such a small amount of cash. How do you juggle your many professional lives and personal life?

> That's a good question. Working in real estate, I have had people scream at me, throw things at me. I'm used to dealing with difficult situations and one thing I've learned early on is that you have to separate your work and your home life. When I'm working on the festival, I'm working on the festival. When I go home at night and I'm hanging out with my girlfriend, I'm not going to bring the festival home with me. I make sure I get sleep every night even if I have something that is due tomorrow. I will sleep because doing stuff without sleep is just wrong.

> So how do I manage the different projects, the different types of careers that I do? Number one is simply not committing to anything you can't do. People

ask me to do things, and if I can't get it done, I just tell him I can't do it. Ask for more time, whatever you need to do.

Number two is follow-through and making sure it happens. One reason I can have the festival is that I have such a great team around me. By using tools like Trollo to track what happens, I am able to work with our director of volunteers, talk with her about things that I think would be great. She can go off and do it, and I can follow up and see how things are going. I hate micro-managing. It's important to let people have freedom but to also set up expectations.

We had some issues with one of our volunteer coordinators last year when she didn't follow through on something that we needed. I blame myself for that because I didn't give her a clear enough picture of what our end goal was. I assumed since she had been in the festival before, she would understand what we needed and that was a mistake. You need to make sure that people understand what you want from them because if you don't, it's your fault if they don't succeed.

So what do you think is your biggest challenge?

We are still new. A good example is that we wanted to screen *Wild* at our film festival and they said, "Why would we want to screen with you?" It's kind of annoying but we are just building our reputation.

A lot of people haven't heard of us, so they are skeptical. But I've been dealing with skepticism my whole life. People have always told me things that I shouldn't be doing, things that I need to do. Sometimes, the advice that people give you is definitely worth listening to and you should do it, but you shouldn't listen to everyone's advice.

At some point, you need to take what you know to be right and do it. When we were deciding upon a name, no one wanted it to be called Portland Film Festival. In fact a friend of mine wanted us to call it "Rose City Film Festival" or "Stumptown Film Festival." It's going to be called Portland Film Festival because there is no other general film festival in Portland with U.S. submissions and international submissions that filmmakers attend. That's what we are selling. People love Portland.

Looking back, would you have changed anything?

I would have. Our first year, it was really hectic and I didn't show my appreciation to the volunteers enough. If I could go back in time, I would have spent more time thanking the volunteers who made the festival happen. We have a lot of return volunteers, which is amazing, but some of the people who gave the most time really burnt out the first year just because they did so much. It was my mistake to not stop them from doing as much as they did. I have this idea that people know their own commitment levels, that you cannot tell them what to do, but really as someone who runs an organization, someone who is older, you need to understand the commitment that is acceptable for your organization. Some people overcommit. You just need to bring them down to a much more manageable commitment level because if you don't, they will burn out and leave.

I agree one hundred percent. Where do you see in your event in three years?

Well, hopefully in another six years, we will be Academy qualifying. Hopefully, we will be growing. I hope to continue to offer more classes and workshops just like any other festival. I would like to screen more films and bring more opportunity to the Portland and Oregon community to learn about film from professionals. I'd love to have more filmmakers come. We are getting submissions from people from our first year. I love supporting our alumni and seeing them grow.

Where do I want to see our festival in the next three years? I would hope that we have more full-time staff.

What are some of the things that you do to spread what little resources you have around, so it looks amazing and people believe that you have a budget that's five to six times the actual number?

You've got to be a little realistic. We don't fly filmmakers out. We tend to only spend money on bringing the press out.

What kind of press? National press?

For us, that's the most important thing.

We're trying to get subsidized housing to start a homestay program for filmmakers if they don't have the money for a hotel. We'll try to find them somewhere to stay but in general, we don't have the money that other festivals do. But we try to make the best events we possibly can.

A lot of it is partnering with people. A lot of our sponsors give us cash, but a lot of them also give us in-kind donations and that really helps. We partner with a lot of film organizations, and we get out to their people. Word of mouth and getting out there and hitting the pavement is key. We have a big street team, and we try to do events that are freaking cool so people want to go. We want to do fun stuff ourselves. We don't want to do boring networking events. We had a networking event for writers in Portland's largest library. We just don't bring someone in to do a boring Q&A.

In the morning, we do a coffee chat. Every director who has a film that plays in the festival is invited that morning at ten o'clock to grab coffee, get in front of the crowd, and talk about his or her film.

What's been your greatest surprise?

The local media is a hard nut to crack. I expected them to be our big supporters and they haven't. We got better press nationally than we have locally. Now don't get me wrong, Oregon's largest newspaper has been great, and they have given us a lot of great press. But the local press, some of these guys I've known for two or three years. They write about us but they are not really invested. That is one of the things that I am really struggling with. What I found last year was having cool events that everyone wants to go to is key.

How do you define success? It could be in relation to the festival, your personal life—anything.

For me, success in life is not stressing over money and surrounding yourself with friends, family, and having loved ones. I don't need to make a certain amount of money to be successful. I don't need a certain type of car. For me, success is being able to do what I love, which is to produce and direct the Portland Film Festival. I love it. It's a passion. I'm very lucky to be able to do something that I truly care about.

How do you define success for the festival?

When the filmmakers have fun. There are some great films I saw and some events I enjoyed. For me, people always worry I am trying to do too much. You need to do less, you need to be quantifiable. You need to screen ten films instead of 145. My whole life, people have always told me what to do, and it really annoys me. I tend to be a person who sits down, looks at the situation and then comes up with a plan and follows through.

Success is the recognition from the attendees that they had a good time. That the filmmakers met someone they hadn't known before and then made a good friendship. To me, the connections, the networking, are what the festival circuits are about. Rare is it that you actually sell a film in the screening. More common is that you will actually meet someone who you are going to work on your next film with. The friendships and partnerships that you can make through the festival circuit are what you should be going after, and it is priceless. The most important people at the festival are the filmmakers.

I'd love Portland to be a destination. I'd love people to want to screen in Portland. Portland's audience is unique because we draw 23 to 40 year-olds. Most festivals typically have older audiences. Our audiences are really a great testing ground for films. If it plays well with us, it's going to play well in theatres throughout the country. We could be a really amazing incubator festival. At Sundance or Toronto, the audience is all film cinephiles. If you put in a short film with a white background, and a guy walking back and forth a thousand times, you know people are going to clap and love that film. Will that actually play to the rest of the world? Maybe not.

What are you most proud of? What contribution do you think will have the biggest, longest lasting impact on the festival?

My biggest contribution is my ability to assemble a network of professionals, films, and filmmakers and bring people together who otherwise never would have come.

What challenges do you see for the future of film festivals in general?

I think relevance. Theater attendance is declining. A lot of films that are created are targeted to male audiences. Festivals are giving movie lovers the diversity that they are not seeing in the studio system. Festivals are becoming more prominent as cultural centers. That's something that festivals have the ability to do and will continue to make them important because curation is important. Look at YouTube. There are tons of shitty videos on YouTube. There are also tons of great videos, but how do you find those great videos? It's through curation. It's through taste and that's what festivals offer. As long as festivals continue to be pioneers and continue to listen to their audiences, they will succeed and they will continue to grow.

And finally, what words of wisdom for someone who wants to start a film festival?

Don't.

You are not the only person who has said that.

> Find a subject you love—find a niche. The reason why the Portland Film Festival could succeed is that the old film festival in town screens 145 films and six of them are from the U.S. So are six U.S. films really a good curation of American films? I don't think so. Last year they had five filmmakers who attended. We had 247. For us, it was about filling a niche that wasn't there. There was no general festival that screened all types of genres and that supports the filmmaker. If your festival can fill a need, then you'll succeed. And then partner, partner, partner. Get as many partners as you can. You can never have too many partners.

RESOURCES

The following list of film festivals and professional resources is by no means complete. Every day, new resources become available. The resource page at reelplan.com is updated regularly to reflect changes and additions.

For those needing consulting services to create, rebrand or refocus a film festival or event, please contact Jon at reelplan.com. If his firm is unable to assist, he is happy to recommend other excellent professionals.

Festivals Created by Interviewees

AFIDocs
AFI DOCS is a five day international documentary film festival that takes place at landmark venues in Washington, DC and the world-class AFI Silver Theatre. With the presence of artists, audience members and political leaders, AFI DOCS shines a bright light on documentary film and harnesses the power of this important art form and its potential to inspire change.
afidocs.com

CineKink
CineKink recognizes and encourages the positive depiction of sexuality and kink in film and television. Featuring a carefully-curated program of films and videos that celebrate and explore the wide diversity of sexuality, with offerings drawn from both Hollywood and beyond, works presented by CineKink range from documentary to drama, camp comedy to artsy experimental, mildly spicy to quite explicit — and everything in between.
cinekink.com

Citizen Jane Film Festival
Citizen Jane Film Festival is an artist's retreat, a holistic experience designed to entertain, enlighten and energize audiences into action and encourage, engage and embolden filmmakers into continuing to ensure that women's stories are told. The festival screens narrative, documentary and short films, hosting panel discussions with the filmmakers.
citizenjanefilmfestival.org

Cucalorus Film Festival
Cucalorus is one of the largest film festivals in the South. More than 200 films screen each year at venues all over downtown Wilmington, attracting over

300 participating artists and thousands of fans and industry professionals. Festival programs focus on dance, music videos, emerging artists, social justice, works-in-progress, and international cinema.
cucalorus.org

DC Shorts Film Festival
Through a series of regularly scheduled educational programs, screening opportunities, sharing resources via online tools, partnering with film, arts and business organizations, and our annual DC Shorts Film Festival, DC Shorts provides opportunities for filmmakers of every skill level to explore and learn their craft — while entertaining and expanding the horizons of audience members.
dcshorts.com

EcoFocus Film Festival
EcoFocus Film Festival is a celebration of environmental films in Athens, Georgia. Our mission is to screen a diversity of high-quality films that promote discussion and inspire audiences into awareness and action on behalf of the environment.
ecofocusfilmfest.org

Edmonton International Film Festival
The Edmonton International Film Festival l is about 'discovery'. We strive to uncover cinematic gems and celebrate unique new voices in independent filmmaking. EIFF is about films and the people who make them. For ten days each autumn, Edmontonians feast on all things cinematic. It's a veritable buffet of the best new indie filmmaking from around the globe. Our schedule includes 55 feature-length slots, and more tan 100 short films programmed into feature-length packages.
edmontonfilmfest.com

GI Film Festival
The GIFF presents films from new and established international and domestic filmmakers that honor the heroic stories of the American Armed Forces and the worldwide struggle for freedom and liberty. Our films express the courage and selflessness of our fighting men and women and the value of their work.
gifilmfestival.com

Holly Shorts Film Festival
HollyShorts is devoted to showcasing the best and brightest short films from around the globe, advancing the careers of filmmakers through screenings,

networking events, and various panel and forums.
hollyshorts.com

Pasadena International Film Festival
Most festivals simply showcase films. The Pasadena International Film Festival creates a unique experience that bridges the worlds of locals, tourists, industry, filmmakers, and businesses. By incorporating movie theatres, live theatre venues, restaurants, lounges, the Public Library, and the Pasadena Museum of History, we fill a void in the film festival circuit.
pasadenafilmfestival.org

Portland Film Festival
The Portland Film Festival is dedicated to nurturing filmmakers and audiences, and to celebrating the power of a good story. The festival focuses on the people, ideas, technology, skills and artistry behind filmmaking and provides both entertaining and educational opportunities to the public and filmmakers.
portlandfilmfestival.com

ReelShorts Film Festival
The Reel Shorts Film Festival celebrates short films and the filmmakers who make them by screening gems of storytelling brilliance from around the world, across Canada, and in the Peace Region.
reelshorts.ca

SF IndieFest
San Francisco Independent Film Festival (SF Indie) runs is an annual festival that showcases the best in independent, alternative, and subversive cinema from around the globe.
sfindie.com

Sidewalk Film Festival
The Sidewalk Film Festival is a celebration of new independent cinema. Since its debut in 1999, filmmakers from across the country and around the world have come to Birmingham, AL to screen their work at Sidewalk and have been thrilled to discover fresh, enthusiastic crowds eager to devour new independent cinema.
sidewalkfest.com

South by Southwest Film Festival
The SXSW Film Festival celebrates raw innovation and emerging talent both

behind and in front of the camera. Featuring provocative documentaries, comedies, genre standouts and more, the festival has become known for the high caliber and diversity of films presented, and for its smart, enthusiastic audiences.
sxsw.com

Tribeca Film Festival
The Tribeca Film Festival is one of the world's leading entertainment platforms, encompassing film premieres, free community events, industry and hospitality programs, VIP opportunities, and a wide range of large scale concerts and events.
tribecafilm.com

WAMMFest
WAMMFest (Women And Minorities in Media Festival) desires to to create more success stories and make a more diverse media industry. Every short work is by or of interest to women and/or minorities, but can and will be enjoyed by anyone. Media makers are encouraged to attend the festival so there can be true interaction between audience and artist
wammtu.com

Woods Hole Film Festival
The Woods Hole Film Festival was established to: organize the annual Festival; form relationships and strategic alliances with other film festivals and organizations to showcase independent film; emphasize the work of emerging and New England filmmakers; showcase the work of independent filmmakers who have a relationship to Cape Cod or whose films are relevant to or enhance the quality of life on Cape Cod and to develop and foster a creative independent film community within the Festival and on Cape Cod.
woodsholefilmfestival.org

National Print and Online Media

Indiewire	indiewire.com
Variety	variety.com
Hollywood Reporter	hollywoodreporter.com
Moviemaker Magazine	moviemaker.com
Filmmaker Magazine	filmmakermagazine.com
FilmFestivals.com	filmfestivals.com

Professional Organizations and Online Discussions

Film Festival Alliance . . . . filmfestivalalliance.org
Film Festival Organizers (Facebook Group)   facebook.com/groups/film-festivalorganizers

Conferences for Film Festival Professionals
Art House Convergence . . . . arthouseconvergence.org
International Film Festival Summit . imfcon.com
FestForward . . . . aboutfest.com

Made in the USA
Charleston, SC
11 December 2015